Social Media Marketing

2024 Edition

By Greg Kihlström

Copyright © 2024 by Greg Kihlström.

All rights reserved. In accordance with the US Copyright Act of 1976, the scanning, uploading, and electronic sharing of any part of this book without the permission of the publisher constitutes unlawful piracy and theft of the author's intellectual property. If you would like to use material from the book (other than for review purposes), prior written permission must be obtained by contacting the author. Thank you for your support of the author's rights.

Published by:

Agile Brand, LLC

3100 Clarendon Boulevard #200, Arlington, VA 22201

https://www.gregkihlstrom.com

First Edition: December 2024

The publisher is not responsible for websites (or their content) that are not owned by the publisher.

Cover design and illustrations by Greg Kihlström

ISBN: 9798303069008

Contents

ACKNOWLEDGEMENTS   5

INTRODUCTION   7

CHAPTER 1: A BRIEF HISTORY OF SOCIAL MEDIA   10

CHAPTER 2: SOCIAL MEDIA AND MARKETING STRATEGY   18

CHAPTER 3: ORGANIC SOCIAL MEDIA   25

CHAPTER 4: PAID SOCIAL MEDIA   32

CHAPTER 5: WHEN TO USE ORGANIC AND PAID SOCIAL   39

CHAPTER 6: EXPLORING INDIVIDUAL SOCIAL MEDIA PLATFORMS   45

CHAPTER 7: FACEBOOK   53

CHAPTER 8: INSTAGRAM   60

CHAPTER 9: TIKTOK   67

CHAPTER 10: YOUTUBE   75

CHAPTER 11: X (FORMERLY TWITTER)   82

CHAPTER 12: LINKEDIN   89

CHAPTER 13: SNAPCHAT 97

CHAPTER 14: OTHER CHANNELS TO CONSIDER 105

CHAPTER 15: SOCIAL COMMERCE 111

CHAPTER 16: CONTENT CREATION BEST PRACTICES FOR SOCIAL MEDIA 117

CHAPTER 17: FUTURE TRENDS IN SOCIAL MEDIA MARKETING TO CONSIDER 124

EPILOGUE 131

ABOUT THE AUTHOR 135

REFERENCES 143

Acknowledgements

As with any book, countless people had a hand in the thoughts and ideas contained within. I will endeavor to thank many of them, but a full list would take up its own book, so please excuse this abbreviated list.

First, I want to thank the many amazing people I work with as an advisor and consultant. I have had the privilege and opportunity to experience many different ways of working, including working firsthand in the area of social media marketing.

Thanks also to my wife Lindsey, who is always supportive of me, no matter how many books I write during the course of a year (this year, it will be three). She is forever an inspiration, and I'm thankful to have such a great partner in all things.

Finally, thank you to everyone reading this book and anyone who has listened to my podcast, read an article, and supported me in any way over the last several years. I hope that the thoughts and ideas shared by myself and others have been helpful in your work.

Let's move forward and create great things together!

Introduction

Social media has evolved from a place to connect with friends and family into one of the most powerful marketing platforms available to brands. What started as a few online communities has become an essential business tool, reshaping the way organizations communicate, build relationships, and sell products to customers. The potential for reach, engagement, and revenue growth is enormous—but to fully harness this potential, businesses must navigate the complexities of an ever-changing landscape.

This book will guide you through the vast ecosystem of social media marketing, offering a strategic blueprint to help your brand rise above the noise. From understanding how social media fits into a broader marketing strategy to mastering the nuances of both organic and paid efforts, you'll learn how to make social media work for your business. Whether you're a seasoned marketer or new to the game, this book is designed to equip you with actionable strategies, platform-specific insights, and an understanding of future trends that will keep your social efforts sharp and relevant.

You'll learn how to create compelling content that resonates, develop a well-rounded approach that leverages the strengths of each platform, and measure the effectiveness of your campaigns with precision. We'll also explore how social commerce is changing the buyer's journey and what businesses need to consider as more consumers look to purchase directly from social platforms.

But social media isn't just about generating likes or shares—it's about building relationships. This book will show you how to transform casual followers into loyal brand advocates and casual scrollers into paying customers.

Social media is constantly evolving, with new platforms, features, and trends emerging at breakneck speed. To stay competitive, marketers need to be adaptable and forward-thinking. By the time you reach the final pages of this book, you'll not only have a comprehensive understanding of today's social media landscape, but you'll also be equipped to anticipate the next wave of changes and capitalize on the opportunities ahead.

Let's dive in and discover how your brand can thrive in the dynamic world of social media marketing.

Chapter 1: A Brief History of Social Media

Before we look at how social media plays a role in the contemporary marketers' goals and strategies, it is helpful to understand where social media came from and the chain of events that has led to the current landscape. Let's take a brief look at this.

The Early Days of Social Platforms

Social media as we know it today didn't begin with Facebook or Instagram. Its roots can be traced back to the early 2000s with platforms like MySpace and Friendster[1]. MySpace, founded in 2003, allowed users to create customizable profiles and connect with friends, becoming one of the first mainstream social networking sites. MySpace quickly became a cultural phenomenon, particularly popular with musicians looking to promote their work. However, its decline came swiftly after the launch of Facebook, which introduced a more user-friendly interface and a stronger focus on real identity and personal networks[2].

Another important precursor to today's social media landscape was Friendster, launched in 2002. Friendster aimed to connect people through mutual friends and was the first platform to introduce the concept of a "social network." However, it struggled with technical issues and was quickly overtaken by competitors, but it laid the groundwork for the social connections that dominate today's online interactions.

The Rise of Facebook and the Social Media Revolution

Facebook, launched in 2004 by Mark Zuckerberg, initially began as a platform for Harvard students but quickly expanded to other universities and eventually the public. It revolutionized social networking by introducing a clean, user-friendly interface and focusing on real-name profiles, which appealed to a broader audience. By 2008, Facebook overtook MySpace as the most visited social media site globally, a title it holds to this day with over 2.6 billion active users[3].

Facebook's success spurred a new era of social media, with more platforms launching to cater to different audiences. Twitter, which launched in 2006, distinguished itself with its short-form updates or "tweets," becoming a hub for real-time communication, especially during events like elections and major news breaks[4].

The Mobile and Visual Era: Instagram and Snapchat

The next significant shift in social media came with the rise of mobile-first platforms. Instagram, launched in 2010, focused on photo sharing and attracted users with its simple interface and visual-first approach. It rapidly gained popularity, reaching one million users within two months and solidifying its place as a major platform after being acquired by Facebook in 2012 for $1 billion[5].

Snapchat, launched in 2011, introduced ephemeral content that disappeared after a short period, a feature that resonated with younger audiences and later inspired features like Instagram Stories. Snapchat's rise marked a shift toward temporary, mobile-friendly content[6].

TikTok and the Short-Form Video Revolution

TikTok, which exploded onto the global scene in 2017, represents the latest major trend in social media: short-form, algorithm-driven video content. TikTok's format encourages creativity and viral trends, making it particularly popular among Gen Z[7]. Its rapid rise underscores the shift toward dynamic, highly engaging content, with over one billion active users globally

The Evolution of Social Media for Businesses

As social media platforms grew, so did their appeal to businesses. Facebook's introduction of paid advertising in 2007 transformed the landscape, allowing businesses to target users based on detailed demographics[8]. This opened the door for other platforms to create business tools, turning social media into a major revenue generator for brands through both organic and paid efforts[9] (

Social Media for Business: A New Era of Marketing

As these platforms grew, so did the opportunities for businesses to market their products and services. The introduction of paid advertising on Facebook in 2007 marked a pivotal shift for brands, allowing them to target users based on detailed demographics and interests This was the beginning of social media's transformation into a serious marketing channel, with businesses investing in both organic content and paid advertising strategies.

Platforms like Instagram and Twitter followed suit, creating business tools and advertising options to help brands reach their audiences. These developments allowed social media marketing to move beyond mere engagement and community building, becoming a key driver of revenue and brand awareness.

Key Moments in Social Media's Evolution for Businesses

Several key moments have shaped social media's journey as a marketing tool:

- 2007: Facebook introduces paid advertising, allowing brands to target users based on detailed demographic data.
- 2013: Instagram launches its advertising platform, making the visually oriented network a hotspot for brands to engage with consumers through photos and videos.

- **2016: Facebook introduces the "live" feature, followed by Instagram, which allows real-time interaction and engagement with audiences.**
- **2019: TikTok becomes the most downloaded app in the world, signaling a shift toward short-form, viral content and redefining how brands engage with Gen Z.**

The Social Media Ecosystem Expands

Over time, new platforms emerged, each offering unique features and capabilities to address the shifting ways that people consumed content. LinkedIn, launched in 2003, became the go-to network for professionals and B2B marketers, focusing on career development, networking, and industry thought leadership.

YouTube, originally founded in 2005 as a video-sharing site, grew into a social network and content creation hub. With the rise of influencers and content creators, YouTube played a pivotal role in the evolution of video as a dominant content format on social media. The introduction of monetization options, such as ads and brand sponsorships, allowed creators to build sustainable careers on the platform, further enhancing its appeal.

The next major phase of social media's evolution came with the rise of visually oriented, mobile-first platforms. Instagram, launched in 2010, focused on photo-sharing, catering to a generation that was increasingly using smartphones to capture and share their experiences. Instagram's focus on high-quality visuals and its later acquisition by Facebook helped it become a cornerstone of many brands' social media strategies.

Around the same time, Snapchat emerged in 2011, offering disappearing photos and videos, a novel concept that appealed to younger users. Snapchat's ephemeral content model pushed other platforms to adopt similar features, such as Instagram's introduction of Stories in 2016, which became one of its most popular features

TikTok, which launched internationally in 2017 (following its predecessor Musical.ly), has since exploded in popularity by focusing on short, engaging videos that encourage creativity and viral trends. TikTok's algorithm-driven content discovery model, which quickly surfaces trending content, has made it the go-to platform for younger audiences and influencers

Conclusion

The history of social media is marked by constant evolution, from the early days of MySpace to the rise of mobile-first and video-driven platforms like Instagram, Snapchat, and

TikTok. These platforms continue to adapt to user behavior and technological advances, offering businesses new ways to connect with their audiences. Understanding this history is crucial for marketers looking to leverage social media effectively and anticipate future trends.

This journey illustrates the fast-paced nature of social media and underscores the need for brands to remain agile and forward-thinking.

Chapter 2: Social Media and Marketing Strategy

Social media has evolved from a novelty to an essential component of any comprehensive marketing strategy. With billions of users on platforms like Facebook, Instagram, and TikTok, businesses that prioritize social media can connect directly with large and diverse audiences, driving significant business outcomes.

1. **Driving Brand Awareness**: Social media allows brands to reach vast audiences quickly and effectively. A recent study by Sprout Social revealed that 55% of consumers learn about new brands via social media By creating shareable content, businesses can increase their visibility and ensure that their brand remains top-of-mind for consumers.

2. **Fostering Engagement**: Unlike traditional marketing channels, social media facilitates two-way conversations, allowing brands to interact with their customers directly. This can foster stronger relationships, as 71% of consumers who have a positive experience with a brand on social media are likely to recommend that brand to others Platforms like Instagram and Twitter enable real-time engagement, making it easier for businesses to respond to customer queries, complaints, or compliments in a timely and public manner.

3. **Lead Generation**: Social media can be a highly effective lead generation tool. Paid campaigns on platforms like LinkedIn and Facebook, for example, can target specific demographics, behaviors, and interests to generate qualified leads. Research shows that 54% of social browsers use social media to research products, indicating that there is significant opportunity to capture potential customers during their discovery phase

4. **Customer Loyalty and Retention**: Beyond customer acquisition, social media plays a key role in customer retention and loyalty. Brands that engage consistently with their audience on social platforms, by providing value through content or resolving issues quickly, can create stronger emotional bonds with their customers. Social media allows businesses to humanize their brand

and foster long-term relationships, leading to repeat purchases and higher customer lifetime value.

Social Media in an Omnichannel World

Social media does not exist in isolation; it functions most effectively when integrated into an omnichannel marketing strategy. In an omnichannel world, customers expect seamless interactions with brands across all touchpoints, including social media, email, content marketing, and offline experiences.

1. **Cross-Channel Consistency**: Social media provides a platform for brands to reinforce messages being delivered through other channels. For instance, a customer might receive an email promotion and later see a retargeted social ad that encourages them to make a purchase. This repetition across channels can increase conversion rates by up to 28%
2. **Retargeting and Journey Mapping**: Platforms like Facebook and Instagram allow businesses to retarget users based on website visits or interactions with previous ads. This helps brands stay connected to users throughout the customer journey, from awareness to conversion. According to a study by HubSpot, retargeted

ads on social media can lead to a 70% higher chance of conversion than non-targeted campaigns

3. **Enhancing Customer Experience**: Social media can enhance the customer journey by offering customer support, product education, and personalized content in real-time. For example, many companies now use chatbots on platforms like Facebook Messenger to provide instant responses to common customer queries. These interactions improve the overall customer experience, providing value at every touchpoint.

4. **Linking Online and Offline Campaigns**: Social media can also be used to bridge the gap between online and offline efforts. For example, brands can use social platforms to promote in-store events or encourage followers to participate in offline experiences, such as product launches or workshops. This integration ensures that the brand remains present throughout both digital and physical touchpoints.

The Rise of the Social Media Team

As the importance of social media has grown, so too has the need for dedicated social media teams within organizations. Initially, social media was often managed by a single person or intern, but it has since evolved into a full-scale department with multiple roles, including community managers, content creators, social strategists, and analysts.

1. **Expanding Social Media Roles**: Today, social media teams often function as an extension of a brand's overall marketing department, collaborating with PR, customer service, and product teams to deliver a cohesive brand message. Social media managers are responsible not only for content creation and posting, but also for managing online communities, analyzing performance data, and aligning social efforts with broader business goals.
2. **Impact on the Business**: A well-resourced social media team can greatly influence a brand's reputation and customer engagement. According to a report by the Content Marketing Institute, 78% of marketers reported that a dedicated social media team is essential to the success of their marketing efforts Social media specialists now play a pivotal role in brand storytelling, real-time marketing, and crisis management, ensuring that the brand's voice is consistent and agile.

Social Media Agencies

Many organizations, particularly small businesses or those lacking in-house resources, turn to external social media agencies to manage their social media presence.

1. **Why Use an Agency?**: External agencies offer specialized expertise, helping businesses develop and execute comprehensive social media strategies. Agencies often bring deep knowledge of the latest platform updates, advertising trends, and analytics tools. They can also provide scalability, allowing businesses to quickly ramp up social efforts during product launches or key campaigns.
2. **Case Studies of Success**: Brands like Wendy's and Nike have worked with agencies to drive successful social media campaigns. Wendy's, for example, gained significant attention for its humorous and engaging Twitter interactions, which were developed in collaboration with its social media agency. This helped the brand generate viral buzz and increase consumer engagement
3. **Full-Service Offerings**: Social media agencies can offer everything from strategy development to content creation, influencer partnerships, and paid ad management. Their ability to provide detailed performance reports and adjust strategies in real-time makes them valuable partners for companies looking to maximize their social media ROI.

Conclusion

Integrating social media into a broader marketing strategy is essential for brands looking to thrive in today's digital landscape. Whether through in-house teams or external agencies, businesses that prioritize social media will find it a powerful tool for building relationships, driving revenue, and enhancing the overall customer experience.

Chapter 3: Organic Social Media

Organic social media refers to content posted without paid promotion, relying on natural reach and engagement from followers. Although paid social media has become increasingly prominent, organic social media remains a key pillar for building lasting relationships, fostering trust, and cultivating an engaged community. To create engaging organic content that resonates with your audience, it's essential to follow best practices centered around community building, storytelling, and leveraging user-generated content.

1. **Community Building**: Successful organic social media strategies revolve around building and nurturing an online community. This involves engaging authentically with followers, responding to comments, and fostering conversations. Brands like Glossier and Starbucks excel

at community building by regularly interacting with their audience, creating a sense of belonging among followers. A dedicated online community increases brand loyalty and turns followers into brand advocates.

2. **Storytelling**: People connect with stories, not just products. Creating compelling narratives around your brand helps humanize it and creates an emotional connection with the audience. Effective storytelling involves sharing behind-the-scenes content, customer success stories, and insights into your brand's values and mission. For instance, brands like Nike often tell stories of athletes overcoming challenges, aligning their message with themes of perseverance and motivation.

3. **User-Generated Content (UGC)**: Encouraging users to create content on your behalf is a powerful way to build trust and authenticity. When followers share their experiences with your product or service, it serves as a form of social proof, making others more likely to engage with your brand. Campaigns like Coca-Cola's "Share a Coke," which encouraged users to post photos of personalized Coke bottles, demonstrate the success of UGC. This type of content tends to drive higher engagement rates as it is perceived as more relatable and authentic.

4. **Consistency and Frequency**: Posting consistently and maintaining a content calendar ensures that your brand

stays top-of-mind without overwhelming your audience. Platforms like Instagram and LinkedIn favor regular activity, and consistent posting helps improve visibility within algorithms. Tools like Hootsuite or Buffer can help brands schedule posts in advance, ensuring consistency in their organic strategy.
5. **Visual Content**: In an age where attention spans are shorter, visually compelling content is essential. High-quality images, infographics, and videos tend to perform better on platforms like Instagram and TikTok, where users expect quick, engaging visuals. Leveraging tools like Canva or Adobe Spark to create on-brand visuals is a best practice for standing out in crowded social media feeds.

How to Measure Organic Success

While organic social media doesn't involve direct ad spend, measuring its success is essential to understand what content works best and to improve performance. Unlike paid media, organic results are often more subtle, but there are several key metrics and tools available to track performance effectively.

1. **Engagement Rates**: Engagement rates measure how users interact with your content, including likes, shares, comments, and clicks. High engagement rates indicate that your content resonates with your audience and

encourages interaction. To calculate engagement rate, divide the total number of interactions by your total number of followers and multiply by 100. Tracking this over time provides insights into what types of posts drive the most engagement.

2. **Reach and Impressions**: Reach refers to the total number of unique users who have seen your content, while impressions reflect the total number of times your content was viewed. Monitoring these metrics helps you understand how far your content is spreading organically. Tools like Facebook Insights and Twitter Analytics provide data on reach and impressions for each post, giving you a clearer picture of organic visibility.

3. **Sentiment Analysis**: Sentiment analysis involves evaluating the tone of the conversations surrounding your brand to determine whether the overall sentiment is positive, neutral, or negative. Social media monitoring tools like Brandwatch and Sprout Social offer sentiment analysis features that allow you to track audience sentiment and identify potential issues before they escalate. Understanding sentiment helps you adjust your content strategy to maintain a positive brand image.

4. **Follower Growth**: Tracking follower growth over time is a basic but essential metric for gauging the effectiveness of your organic content. A steady increase

in followers typically indicates that your content is attracting new audiences, while stagnation might suggest the need for a strategy refresh. Monitoring where your followers are coming from (e.g., direct search, word-of-mouth, or hashtags) can provide insights into which tactics are driving growth.

5. **Customer Feedback and Conversations**: Organic social media is a valuable tool for gathering real-time feedback from your audience. Monitoring comments, mentions, and direct messages allows you to gauge how customers feel about your products or services. Tools like Mention and Hootsuite track brand mentions across platforms, helping you stay informed about customer sentiment and conversations.

6. **Tools and Methodologies**: Several platforms and tools provide the data you need to measure the success of your organic efforts:
    - **Native Analytics Tools**: Most social media platforms offer built-in analytics to track organic performance. For example, Instagram Insights allows users to track engagement, reach, impressions, and follower demographics. Similarly, LinkedIn Analytics offers detailed insights into post performance and audience data.

- **Third-Party Tools**: Tools like Sprout Social, Hootsuite, and Buffer provide comprehensive dashboards for tracking performance across multiple platforms. These tools often include additional features like sentiment analysis, competitor benchmarking, and advanced reporting.
- **Google Analytics**: Tracking website traffic from social media sources in Google Analytics helps you measure the impact of social content on driving traffic to your website. Monitoring referral traffic from social media provides insights into how well your content motivates users to take action.

By focusing on these key metrics and employing the right tools, you can ensure that your organic social media strategy is aligned with your business goals and continuously optimized for better results.

Conclusion

Organic social media, when executed with strategic content creation and effective measurement practices, remains a critical piece of any successful marketing strategy. While it may not deliver immediate results like paid campaigns, the long-term benefits of building authentic relationships, fostering community, and maintaining brand visibility make it a worthwhile investment.

Chapter 4: Paid Social Media

Paid social media has transformed the way brands reach and engage with audiences, offering precise targeting, measurable results, and unparalleled scalability. While organic social media helps brands build trust and community, paid social media accelerates visibility and drives specific actions, such as purchases or sign-ups. Whether through Facebook Ads, Instagram's shoppable posts, or LinkedIn's sponsored content, paid social campaigns have become a central pillar in modern marketing strategies.

Origins of Paid Social Media

The rise of paid social media began with Facebook's introduction of advertising on its platform in 2007. Initially, brands used Facebook Ads to promote their pages and increase likes. Over time, Facebook refined its targeting capabilities, offering advertisers more sophisticated tools to reach audiences based on demographics, interests, and behaviors. By 2012, Facebook introduced the ability to promote posts directly in users' newsfeeds, blending organic and paid content in a more seamless way

Other platforms followed suit, with Twitter introducing Promoted Tweets in 2010, allowing advertisers to insert their content into users' feeds, while LinkedIn launched sponsored updates in 2013. These early approaches to paid social media set the stage for the highly targeted and data-driven ad campaigns we see today, where businesses can reach niche audiences with tailored messages across multiple platforms.

Best Practices for Paid Social Campaigns

1. **Audience Segmentation**: The key to effective paid social campaigns lies in targeting the right audience. Platforms like Facebook and Instagram allow for granular segmentation based on demographics, behaviors, and interests. Audience segmentation ensures that your ads reach users who are most likely to engage with your brand or product. Additionally, tools like Facebook's Lookalike Audiences enable advertisers to target users who share similarities with their existing customers, maximizing the effectiveness of the ad spend.

2. **A/B Testing**: A/B testing (also called split testing) is a crucial strategy for optimizing paid social campaigns. By testing different variations of an ad—whether it's the image, copy, or call-to-action—brands can gather data on what resonates best with their audience. For example, advertisers can test two different headlines to see which generates a higher click-through rate (CTR). Regular A/B testing helps fine-tune campaign performance and drive better results.

3. **Creative Design**: Creative design plays a significant role in the success of paid social media. Ads should be visually appealing, consistent with the brand's overall image, and optimized for the specific platform. For example, Instagram ads often perform best with high-quality images or short videos, while LinkedIn ads may focus more on professional messaging and less on visuals. Ensuring your ad creative aligns with the platform's user expectations is critical for engagement.

4. **Budget Management**: Managing the budget effectively ensures that campaigns are not only cost-efficient but also impactful. Paid social platforms offer a variety of bidding strategies, including cost-per-click (CPC) or cost-per-impression (CPM), allowing advertisers to control how much they are willing to spend to achieve their goals. It's important to monitor spending regularly and adjust budgets based on performance. Scaling

campaigns that show strong results and pausing underperforming ones can optimize return on investment.
5. **Retargeting**: Retargeting is an essential tactic in paid social campaigns, allowing brands to serve ads to users who have already interacted with their website or content. Platforms like Facebook and Google enable retargeting based on pixel data, ensuring that ads are shown to users who are familiar with the brand. Retargeting often leads to higher conversion rates, as these users have already demonstrated interest in the brand.

How to Measure Paid Social ROI

To measure the success of paid social media campaigns, it's crucial to track a range of metrics. These metrics provide insight into how well the campaigns are driving business objectives and allow for ongoing optimization.

1. **Return on Ad Spend (ROAS)**: ROAS measures the revenue generated for every dollar spent on advertising. It's one of the most critical metrics for understanding the profitability of paid social campaigns. For example, a ROAS of 3:1 means that for every dollar spent on ads, three dollars in revenue are generated. To improve ROAS, advertisers should continually optimize

targeting, creative, and bidding strategies based on performance data.

2. **Cost per Acquisition (CPA)**: CPA tracks the cost of acquiring a new customer through paid social ads. It's calculated by dividing the total ad spend by the number of conversions. A low CPA indicates efficient spending, while a high CPA might suggest that the targeting or creative needs improvement. Lowering CPA should be a key focus of any paid social media strategy.

3. **Click-Through Rate (CTR)**: CTR measures the percentage of users who click on an ad after seeing it. A higher CTR indicates that the ad is relevant and engaging to the audience. Tracking CTR helps advertisers assess the effectiveness of their ad copy, creative, and targeting. Ads with low CTR might require adjustments to improve their appeal.

4. **Conversion Rate**: Conversion rate refers to the percentage of users who complete a desired action (e.g., making a purchase or signing up for a newsletter) after clicking on an ad. This metric is critical for measuring how well paid social campaigns are driving tangible business results. Optimizing landing pages and ensuring a smooth user experience after the click can improve conversion rates.

5. **Cost per Click (CPC)**: CPC measures how much an advertiser pays for each click on their ad. While CPC

alone doesn't indicate success, tracking it in combination with CTR and conversion rate can give a clearer picture of overall performance. A low CPC with a high conversion rate often indicates a successful campaign.

6. **Impressions and Reach**: While impressions refer to the number of times an ad is displayed, reach counts the unique users who see it. Monitoring these metrics is useful for understanding how far your ad is spreading and ensuring it's reaching the intended audience. High impressions with low engagement may indicate ad fatigue or irrelevant targeting.

Conclusion

Paid social media has evolved into a powerful tool for brands looking to expand their reach, generate leads, and drive revenue. From its early beginnings with Facebook Ads to today's multi-platform, data-driven campaigns, paid social offers unprecedented targeting and flexibility. By following best practices in audience segmentation, A/B testing, creative design, and budget management, businesses can craft effective campaigns that deliver measurable ROI. Monitoring key metrics like ROAS, CPA, and CTR ensures that paid social efforts are optimized for success, allowing brands to scale their marketing impact in an increasingly competitive digital landscape.

Chapter 5: When to use Organic and Paid Social

Organic and paid social media are two sides of the same coin, each playing a vital role in building a strong digital presence. While organic social media focuses on building trust, community, and authentic connections, paid social media accelerates reach and drives specific actions. Understanding when to use each—and how to combine them effectively—can help marketers maximize the impact of their campaigns while staying efficient with time and resources. This chapter explores the strengths of organic and paid strategies, when to prioritize one over the other, and how to create a winning combination of the two.

When to Use Organic Instead of Paid

Organic social media is the foundation of a strong online presence, providing a platform for consistent engagement with followers without the need for a financial investment. It's particularly effective in the following scenarios:

1. **Building Brand Awareness Over Time**: Organic content is ideal for nurturing long-term relationships with your audience. Regular posts, community interactions, and user-generated content help establish your brand's personality and build trust.
   Example: Patagonia excels in organic social media by sharing posts about sustainability and environmental causes, reinforcing its brand mission while connecting with like-minded audiences.
2. **Engaging with Existing Followers**: Organic social media is perfect for keeping your existing audience engaged. Through polls, comments, Stories, and behind-the-scenes content, brands can foster meaningful interactions with their followers.
3. **Launching New Content or Ideas**: Testing new content types or campaign ideas organically allows you to gauge audience interest before committing to a paid strategy. Organic feedback can inform adjustments and improvements.
4. **Demonstrating Authenticity**: Organic posts allow brands to share stories, respond to followers, and

showcase their human side. This authenticity helps build trust, which is essential for customer loyalty.

When to Use Paid Instead of Organic

Paid social media is a powerful way to amplify reach, target specific audiences, and achieve measurable business goals quickly. It's particularly effective in the following situations:

1. **Reaching a Wider Audience**: Organic reach has declined on most platforms due to algorithm changes. Paid campaigns ensure your content is seen by users who are not already following your page, especially when targeting specific demographics.
   Example: A local fitness studio can use paid ads to target users within a specific geographic area interested in health and wellness.
2. **Driving Immediate Conversions**: Paid social media is best for promoting time-sensitive offers, such as sales, product launches, or events. Ads with clear calls-to-action (CTAs) can drive traffic, leads, and sales more efficiently than organic posts.
3. **Testing and Scaling Campaigns**: Paid campaigns allow you to test different creatives, audiences, and messages in real-time. Once a strategy proves successful, you can scale it quickly to maximize results.

4. **Competing in Crowded Markets**: For industries with high competition, paid ads are essential to ensure your brand stands out. Precise targeting options and retargeting features can help you capture attention and drive engagement.

How Both Can Work Together

The real power of social media lies in combining organic and paid strategies to create a cohesive and impactful marketing plan. Here's how they can complement each other:

1. **Amplify High-Performing Organic Content**: Use paid ads to boost organic posts that have already shown strong engagement. This ensures your best-performing content reaches a larger audience.
   Example: A restaurant shares a video of its signature dish that performs well organically. Boosting the post ensures it reaches potential customers beyond its followers.
2. **Build an Organic Presence Before Paid**: Establishing an organic social media presence builds credibility. When you start running paid ads, users will check your profile to verify your legitimacy. A strong organic presence makes a positive first impression.
3. **Retarget Organic Visitors with Paid Ads**: Organic content often attracts visitors who don't take immediate

action. Use retargeting ads to remind these visitors about your brand and encourage conversions.
4. **Create a Customer Journey**: Organic content nurtures relationships, while paid campaigns drive specific actions. Together, they create a seamless customer journey from awareness to purchase.

Tips for Success

To get the most out of organic and paid social media, consider these tips:

1. **Define Clear Objectives**: Understand the goals of each campaign. Use organic content for engagement and community-building, and paid ads for lead generation and conversions.
2. **Leverage Data for Decision-Making**: Analyze performance metrics for both organic and paid campaigns. Use insights to optimize your strategy and allocate resources effectively.
3. **Stay Consistent**: Maintain a consistent brand voice across both organic and paid efforts to ensure your audience experiences a cohesive message.
4. **Adapt to Platform Trends**: Keep an eye on platform updates and emerging trends. Experiment with new features (like Reels or TikTok ads) to stay relevant.

5. **Test and Iterate**: Continuously test different types of content, targeting options, and ad formats to identify what resonates most with your audience.

Conclusion

Organic and paid social media are not mutually exclusive; they are complementary strategies that, when combined, can create a powerful marketing engine. By understanding when to prioritize one over the other and how to use them together, brands can maximize their reach, engagement, and ROI. The key is to remain adaptable, data-driven, and focused on delivering value to your audience. In the ever-evolving world of social media, a balanced approach to organic and paid strategies ensures that your brand remains visible, competitive, and impactful.

Chapter 6: Exploring Individual Social Media Platforms

Social media platforms are as diverse as the audiences they serve. From Instagram's visually driven culture to LinkedIn's professional networking focus, each platform has unique strengths and audience demographics. However, not every platform is the right fit for every business. Choosing where to invest your time, energy, and resources can determine the success of your social media strategy. This chapter explores how to evaluate platforms, find where your customers are, and build a focused, effective presence that aligns with your business goals.

Each social media platform has its own unique features, user base, and content strategies that make it suitable for different types of marketing efforts. Understanding the nuances of each platform is essential for marketers to effectively tailor their campaigns, maximize engagement, and achieve business goals. In this section, we will explore the major social media platforms—Facebook, Instagram, TikTok, YouTube, X (formerly Twitter), and LinkedIn—discussing their tools, best practices, and audience demographics. We'll also touch on emerging platforms and niche social networks that marketers should consider.

- **Facebook**
  Overview of Facebook's tools, advertising options, and organic content strategies. Discuss audience demographics and best practices.
- **Instagram**
  Focus on Instagram's visual storytelling, Reels, Stories, and influencer collaborations. Offer tips on leveraging Instagram for brand building and e-commerce.
- **TikTok**
  Discuss TikTok's viral nature, its short-form content strategy, and how brands can use trends and challenges to engage with younger audiences.
- **YouTube**
  Guide on video content creation, SEO for YouTube, and how brands can build communities and trust through long-form video.
- **X (formerly Twitter)**
  Discuss Twitter's strengths in real-time engagement,

customer service, and thought leadership. Offer insights on content curation and campaign strategies.

- **LinkedIn**

  Focus on B2B marketing, personal branding, and LinkedIn Ads. Explore content formats such as posts, articles, and video.

- **Snapchat**

  Focus on short video content and engaging with younger audiences.

- **Other Channels to Consider**

  Of course, there are many more platforms to consider, including mainstream ones such as Pinterest, Threads, and Bluesky, as well as niche platforms that focus on specific industries.

Determining the Best Fit for Your Business

Not all social media platforms will align with your business objectives, target audience, or brand personality. To determine the best fit, consider the following factors:

1. **Audience Demographics**: Evaluate who uses the platform. Instagram skews younger, LinkedIn is ideal for B2B professionals, and Pinterest appeals to creatives and

shoppers. Choose platforms where your target audience is most active.

2. **Content Format**: Some platforms excel in specific content types. For example, TikTok thrives on short-form videos, while Twitter is better suited for quick updates and thought leadership. Match your platform choice to your strengths and the content formats your audience engages with.

3. **Business Objectives**: Define your goals. If brand awareness is the priority, platforms like Instagram or TikTok may be the best choice. For lead generation or B2B networking, LinkedIn could be more effective.

4. **Advertising Capabilities**: Consider the advertising options each platform offers. Facebook and Instagram have advanced targeting tools, while TikTok and Pinterest are growing their paid ad offerings.

5. **Competition and Trends**: Research what platforms your competitors are using successfully. Their presence can provide insights into where your industry thrives.

Finding Where Your Customers Are

The foundation of an effective social media strategy is being present where your customers already spend their time. To identify the right platforms, you'll need to:

1. **Research Audience Preferences**: Use customer surveys, industry reports, and platform-specific audience insights to understand where your target market engages most. For instance, Gen Z is heavily active on TikTok, while older demographics lean toward Facebook.
2. **Monitor Customer Behavior**: Look for patterns in how customers interact with your brand. Are they tagging your business in Instagram Stories? Do they leave product reviews on Pinterest? These behaviors signal platform preference.
3. **Analyze Competitor Activity**: Observe where your competitors are active and successful. If a competitor consistently generates engagement on LinkedIn, it may indicate an opportunity for your brand to do the same.
4. **Use Analytics Tools**: Platforms like Google Analytics and social media monitoring tools can reveal referral traffic sources and customer activity by platform.

Don't Be All Things to Everyone

Spreading your efforts across too many platforms dilutes your impact. A focused presence on a few platforms is far more effective than a scattered approach across many. Here's why:

1. **Quality Over Quantity**: Creating high-quality content tailored to one or two platforms will yield better results than generic content spread across multiple channels.

2. **Audience Expectation**: Users expect unique, tailored experiences on each platform. Attempting to manage too many platforms often leads to content that feels out of place or uninspired.
3. **Brand Consistency**: Concentrating your efforts allows you to maintain a consistent voice, tone, and aesthetic, which builds trust and recognition.

   Example: A boutique fashion brand may find success focusing solely on Instagram and Pinterest, where visual storytelling and shopping integration thrive, rather than trying to maintain a presence on LinkedIn or Twitter.

Expand When You Have the Resources to Do So

Once you've mastered a few platforms and have the resources to expand, consider broadening your social media footprint. However, expansion should be strategic:

1. **Evaluate ROI**: Determine if your existing platforms are delivering measurable results. Expansion should only occur if the effort and budget required to manage additional platforms will lead to incremental gains.
2. **Build a Plan**: Before expanding, create a clear strategy for the new platform, including content types, posting frequency, and goals.

3. **Scale Your Team**: Managing multiple platforms requires more resources, including time, creative assets, and personnel. Ensure your team can handle the added workload without sacrificing quality.
4. **Leverage Automation Tools**: Tools like Hootsuite or Buffer can streamline posting and analytics, making it easier to manage multiple accounts.

Continually Test and Experiment: Consumer Habits Change

Consumer behavior on social media is constantly evolving, driven by new trends, features, and platforms. Staying relevant requires ongoing experimentation and adaptation:

1. **Try New Platforms**: Emerging platforms like Threads or niche networks may provide untapped opportunities. Test them on a small scale before fully committing.
2. **Experiment with Features**: Social platforms frequently roll out new tools, such as Instagram Reels or TikTok Shopping. Early adopters often benefit from higher visibility and engagement.
3. **Monitor Trends**: Stay informed about shifting trends, such as the rise of social commerce or the popularity of short-form video content. Adapt your strategy accordingly.

4. **Analyze Results**: Use platform analytics and A/B testing to identify what works best. Testing variations of content types, posting times, and messaging can yield valuable insights.

Conclusion

Choosing the right social media platforms for your business isn't about being everywhere—it's about being where your customers are and where your brand can shine. By focusing on the platforms that align with your goals and audience, maintaining a consistent presence, and staying adaptable to changes in consumer behavior, you can build a social media strategy that delivers meaningful results.

In the pages that follow, we'll explore some of the most popular social media platforms so you can start assessing which will be the best fit for your business. Remember, social media success lies not in spreading yourself thin but in making a deep, impactful connection with your audience where it matters most.

Chapter 7: Facebook

With over 3 billion monthly active users, Facebook remains a cornerstone of social media marketing. Its vast user base, sophisticated targeting tools, and robust advertising capabilities make it a go-to platform for businesses of all sizes[10]. Whether you're aiming to build a community, drive engagement, or boost sales, Facebook offers tools and features that can help you achieve your goals. This chapter dives into how to leverage Facebook effectively, from understanding its audience to optimizing organic and paid strategies.

Audience Demographics

Facebook's user base spans multiple age groups, offering broad appeal for both B2C and B2B marketers. While younger audiences are increasingly turning to platforms like TikTok and Instagram, Facebook remains highly relevant for engaging with older demographics:

- **Age Groups**: The platform is particularly strong among adults aged 25-34, while users aged 35+ represent a significant portion of its audience. It is also popular among Gen X and Baby Boomers, making it a versatile choice for businesses targeting diverse age groups.
- **Global Reach**: Facebook's users are distributed globally, with large populations in North America, Europe, and Asia, making it ideal for international campaigns.
- **B2C and B2B Appeal**: While Facebook is widely used for B2C marketing, its audience includes professionals and business decision-makers, providing opportunities for B2B marketers as well.

Understanding these demographics can help businesses tailor their messaging and strategy to resonate with the right audience.

Content Best Practices

Creating content that sparks engagement is key to succeeding on Facebook, as its algorithm prioritizes posts that generate meaningful interactions.

1. **Encourage Engagement**: Use questions, polls, and calls to action (CTAs) to prompt users to comment, react, or share your content.

2. **Leverage Facebook Groups**: Groups are an excellent way to build a sense of community around your brand. Engaging directly with members in a group fosters trust and loyalty.
3. **Post Videos**: Facebook favors video content, particularly live videos, which often receive higher visibility and engagement. Use videos to tell stories, demonstrate products, or host live Q&A sessions.
4. **Use User-Generated Content (UGC)**: Showcase photos, videos, or testimonials from your customers to build trust and authenticity.
5. **Consistency**: Post regularly and maintain a consistent tone and aesthetic that aligns with your brand.

Using Facebook for Organic Social Media Marketing

Organic social media on Facebook is centered around building relationships and engaging with followers without relying on paid promotion.

- **Community Building**: Use features like Facebook Groups to connect with your audience in a meaningful way. Groups allow members to interact with your brand and each other, creating a loyal community.

- **Educational Content**: Share articles, infographics, and how-to guides that provide value to your audience. Informative posts position your brand as a trusted resource.
- **Event Promotion**: Facebook Events are a great tool for organic outreach, allowing you to invite followers to virtual or in-person gatherings, webinars, or product launches.

Paid Social Media Functionality

Facebook Ads Manager offers a comprehensive suite of tools for creating and managing paid campaigns. Its advanced targeting options make it one of the most powerful advertising platforms available.

1. **Advanced Targeting**: Target users based on demographics, interests, behaviors, and even life events (e.g., birthdays or upcoming anniversaries).
2. **Custom and Lookalike Audiences**: Use Custom Audiences to target existing customers or Lookalike Audiences to reach new users similar to your customer base.
3. **Ad Formats**: Facebook supports a variety of ad formats, including image ads, video ads, carousel ads, and lead generation ads, catering to diverse marketing goals.

4. **Budget Flexibility**: Whether you have a small or large budget, Facebook allows you to scale campaigns based on your resources.
5. **Retargeting**: Use Facebook Pixel to retarget users who have visited your website or engaged with your content but haven't converted yet.

Key Metrics to Measure Success

Tracking performance is essential to optimizing your strategy. Facebook provides robust analytics tools for monitoring campaign performance and organic reach.

1. **Engagement Rate**: Measure likes, shares, and comments to assess how well your content resonates with your audience.
2. **Reach and Impressions**: Track how many users see your posts and how often your content is displayed.
3. **Click-Through Rate (CTR)**: Evaluate the effectiveness of your CTAs and ad copy.
4. **Conversions**: Monitor actions taken as a result of your campaigns, such as purchases, sign-ups, or downloads.
5. **Return on Ad Spend (ROAS)**: Calculate the revenue generated for every dollar spent on advertising.

Checklist of 10 Tips to Be Successful on Facebook

1. **Define Clear Goals**: Determine whether your focus is on awareness, engagement, or conversions.
2. **Know Your Audience**: Use analytics to understand demographics and tailor content accordingly.
3. **Post Consistently**: Create a content calendar and stick to a regular posting schedule.
4. **Engage with Followers**: Respond to comments and messages promptly to build relationships.
5. **Leverage Video Content**: Incorporate live streams, tutorials, and behind-the-scenes footage.
6. **Boost High-Performing Posts**: Use paid ads to amplify successful organic content.
7. **Experiment with Ad Formats**: Test different ad types to see what works best for your goals.
8. **Use Retargeting**: Re-engage users who interacted with your website or posts.
9. **Analyze Performance**: Regularly review metrics to identify strengths and areas for improvement.
10. **Stay Current**: Monitor platform updates and algorithm changes to adapt your strategy.

Conclusion

Facebook's versatility, expansive user base, and advanced advertising tools make it a critical platform for businesses aiming to build a strong online presence. By understanding the platform's audience, leveraging both organic and paid strategies, and tracking key metrics, brands can drive meaningful engagement and achieve measurable results. Whether you're fostering a loyal community or scaling your advertising efforts, Facebook offers unparalleled opportunities for businesses ready to adapt and thrive in the dynamic social media landscape.

Chapter 8: Instagram

With over 2 billion monthly active users, Instagram has become a visual powerhouse for brands seeking to connect with audiences through storytelling, lifestyle content, and e-commerce[11]. Known for its focus on high-quality imagery and videos, Instagram offers a suite of features—from Reels to Stories and Shoppable Posts—that cater to both engagement and sales. This chapter explores how to make the most of Instagram by understanding its audience, leveraging its content formats, and integrating organic and paid strategies for maximum impact.

Audience Demographics

Instagram's user base is younger and more visually oriented, making it an ideal platform for brands targeting millennials, Gen Z, and lifestyle-focused consumers:

- **Age Groups**: Instagram's core demographic is users aged 18-34, though it also attracts a growing audience in the 35-44 age range.
- **Global Reach**: The platform has a strong international presence, particularly in North America, Europe, and parts of Asia.
- **Gender Distribution**: Instagram skews slightly female, with women accounting for approximately 52% of its user base.
- **Interest Areas**: Popular categories on Instagram include fashion, beauty, travel, fitness, food, and lifestyle, making it ideal for brands in these industries.

Content Best Practices

Success on Instagram hinges on creating visually compelling content that resonates with your audience while staying consistent with your brand identity.

1. **Maintain a Cohesive Aesthetic**: Your Instagram profile serves as a virtual storefront, and a consistent color palette, tone, and style make a lasting impression. Tools like Adobe Lightroom and Canva can help standardize your visuals.
2. **Leverage Reels**: Reels are Instagram's short-form video feature, ideal for sharing entertaining, trend-driven

content. Use trending audio, creative transitions, and relatable storytelling to maximize reach.
3. **Engage with Stories**: Stories provide a more casual, real-time way to interact with followers. Use polls, quizzes, stickers, and behind-the-scenes content to increase engagement.
4. **Showcase User-Generated Content (UGC)**: Reposting UGC not only saves time but also builds trust and community by showcasing real customers using your products.
5. **Highlight Your Products**: Use high-quality images and videos to showcase your products in action, with clear CTAs encouraging users to explore further.

Using Instagram for Organic Social Media Marketing

Organic content is the heart of Instagram, offering opportunities to build brand loyalty, foster community, and showcase authenticity.

- **Storytelling Through Posts**: Share content that reflects your brand's values and mission. For instance, a sustainable fashion brand might post about its ethical sourcing practices alongside visually appealing product shots.

- **Interactive Features in Stories**: Use interactive tools like polls, quizzes, and "Ask Me Anything" stickers to engage directly with your audience and gather valuable insights.
- **Build Relationships Through DMs**: Direct messages provide a personal way to connect with followers, answer questions, and resolve customer inquiries.
- **Grow with Hashtags**: Strategic use of hashtags increases discoverability. Combine branded hashtags with popular industry-related ones to reach new audiences.

Paid Social Media Functionality

Instagram's advertising capabilities allow brands to amplify their reach, target specific audiences, and drive measurable results.

1. **Ad Formats**: Instagram supports various ad types, including photo ads, video ads, carousel ads, Stories ads, and Reels ads. Each format caters to different marketing goals, from brand awareness to conversions.
2. **Targeting Options**: Using Facebook Ads Manager, advertisers can target Instagram users based on demographics, interests, behaviors, and even lookalike audiences.

3. **Shoppable Posts and Ads**: Businesses can use Instagram Shopping to create shoppable posts, making it easy for users to purchase directly from the platform. Shoppable ads amplify product visibility, driving traffic to specific items.
4. **Influencer Collaborations**: Paid partnerships with influencers expand your reach by leveraging their established audiences. Use the "Paid Partnership" tag to maintain transparency and track performance.

Key Metrics to Measure Success

Tracking performance on Instagram ensures that your efforts align with business goals. Focus on these metrics:

1. **Engagement Rate**: Measure likes, comments, shares, and saves to gauge how well your content resonates with followers.
2. **Impressions and Reach**: Monitor how many people see your posts and how often they are displayed.
3. **Click-Through Rate (CTR)**: Evaluate the effectiveness of your CTAs in ads and shoppable posts.
4. **Follower Growth**: Track how your audience expands over time to assess the long-term impact of your strategy.
5. **Conversions**: Measure actions like purchases, website visits, or sign-ups driven by your Instagram content.

Checklist of 10 Tips to Be Successful on Instagram

1. **Define Your Brand Aesthetic**: Maintain a consistent look and feel across all posts.
2. **Use High-Quality Visuals**: Invest in professional photography or design tools to create polished content.
3. **Post Regularly**: Maintain a consistent posting schedule to keep your audience engaged.
4. **Engage with Followers**: Respond to comments and DMs promptly to foster relationships.
5. **Leverage Reels and Stories**: Use these features to create dynamic, engaging content.
6. **Collaborate with Influencers**: Partner with influencers to expand your reach authentically.
7. **Utilize Hashtags Strategically**: Use a mix of branded and popular hashtags to increase discoverability.
8. **Test Ad Formats**: Experiment with different ad types to identify what drives the best results.
9. **Analyze Insights**: Use Instagram Insights to track performance and optimize your strategy.
10. **Stay Updated on Trends**: Monitor changes in Instagram features and adapt your approach accordingly.

Conclusion

Instagram's focus on visual storytelling, engagement-driven features, and seamless shopping integration makes it a powerful platform for businesses across industries. By understanding your audience, crafting high-quality content, and leveraging both organic and paid strategies, you can build a strong presence that drives meaningful connections and measurable results. Whether you're showcasing lifestyle content, promoting products, or fostering community, Instagram provides the tools to elevate your brand in the digital space.

Chapter 9: TikTok

TikTok has become a cultural phenomenon, attracting over 1.6 billion active users and redefining how content is created and consumed[12]. Known for its short-form, highly engaging videos, TikTok thrives on trends, challenges, and creativity. For brands, it offers an unparalleled opportunity to connect with younger audiences through authentic and entertaining content. This chapter explores how to leverage TikTok effectively, from understanding its audience to crafting strategies for organic growth and paid campaigns.

Audience Demographics

TikTok's user base is dominated by younger generations, making it a prime platform for brands targeting Gen Z and millennials:

- **Age Groups**: Over 60% of TikTok's users are under 30, with the largest demographic being 18-24 years old. However, its popularity among older audiences is steadily increasing.
- **Global Reach**: TikTok has a massive international presence, with strong adoption in North America, Europe, and Asia.
- **Interests and Behaviors**: TikTok users are highly engaged, spending an average of 95 minutes per day on the platform. They are drawn to creative, relatable, and often humorous content, making the platform ideal for brands that embrace an informal tone.

Content Best Practices

Creating successful content on TikTok requires a blend of creativity, authenticity, and relevance to platform trends. Here's how to stand out:

1. **Focus on Trends**: TikTok is trend-driven, so staying updated on trending sounds, hashtags, and challenges is essential. Participating in trends increases the likelihood of your content being featured on the For You Page (FYP).
2. **Prioritize Authenticity**: TikTok users value authenticity over polished production. Showcasing behind-the-scenes

footage, employee stories, or raw, unfiltered moments often resonates more than professionally produced ads.
3. **Make an Impact Quickly**: The first few seconds of a video are critical. Use eye-catching visuals, bold text overlays, or an intriguing question to hook viewers immediately.
4. **Leverage User-Generated Content (UGC)**: Encourage your audience to create content using your products or services, often through branded challenges or giveaways.
5. **Use Vertical Video Format**: TikTok videos are optimized for vertical viewing. Ensure all content is formatted to fit the platform's dimensions for maximum engagement.

Using TikTok for Organic Social Media Marketing

Organic content on TikTok is all about building relationships and fostering engagement through creativity and relatability:

- **Participate in Challenges**: Challenges are a cornerstone of TikTok culture. Brands can join trending challenges or create their own branded challenges to engage users and encourage UGC.

- **Tap Into Storytelling**: Use short-form storytelling to highlight your brand's mission, showcase customer success stories, or demonstrate how your product solves a problem.
- **Educate and Entertain**: Informative videos (e.g., tutorials, tips, or how-tos) that also entertain tend to perform well. For example, a skincare brand might share quick, engaging skincare routines.
- **Collaborate With Creators**: Partnering with TikTok influencers can help amplify your message and reach new audiences authentically.
- **Be Consistent**: Posting regularly (e.g., 3-5 times per week) helps maintain visibility and engagement on the platform.

Paid Social Media Functionality

TikTok's advertising options allow brands to amplify their reach and drive measurable results through creative campaigns.

1. **Ad Formats**:
    - **In-Feed Ads**: These ads appear within a user's feed and feel like native content.
    - **Branded Hashtag Challenges**: Encourage users to participate in a challenge centered around

your brand, creating massive visibility and UGC.
   - **Branded Effects**: Create custom AR filters or effects that users can interact with, fostering engagement.
   - **TopView Ads**: These premium placements appear when users open the app, ensuring high visibility.
   - **Spark Ads**: Amplify existing organic content, either from your brand or from creators who've featured your product.
2. **Targeting Options**: TikTok's algorithm offers advanced targeting based on demographics, interests, device types, and behaviors. Lookalike audiences allow brands to reach users similar to their existing customers.
3. **Budget Flexibility**: Campaigns can be scaled to fit any budget, from small businesses testing their first ads to large-scale product launches.

Key Metrics to Measure Success

Tracking performance on TikTok is essential to refining your strategy and ensuring ROI. Focus on these key metrics:

1. **Engagement Rate**: Monitor likes, shares, comments, and saves to evaluate how well your content resonates.

2. **Reach and Impressions**: Track how many unique users view your videos and how often they're displayed.
3. **Completion Rate**: Measure the percentage of users who watch your video to the end—a critical metric for content effectiveness.
4. **Hashtag Performance**: If running a branded hashtag challenge, measure how many users participate and the reach of your hashtag.
5. **Conversions**: For ads, track actions like website visits, sign-ups, or purchases resulting from your campaigns.

Checklist of 10 Tips to Be Successful on TikTok

1. **Understand the Culture**: Immerse yourself in TikTok trends and humor to create content that feels native to the platform.
2. **Be Authentic**: Showcase real people and relatable moments rather than polished corporate content.
3. **Focus on Trends**: Use trending sounds, hashtags, and challenges to increase visibility.
4. **Collaborate with Creators**: Partner with TikTok influencers to expand your reach authentically.
5. **Create Short, Engaging Videos**: Hook viewers within the first few seconds to ensure they watch your content.

6. **Leverage UGC**: Encourage your audience to create content around your brand or participate in challenges.
7. **Experiment with Ad Formats**: Test different TikTok ad types to identify what works best for your goals.
8. **Post Consistently**: Stay active on the platform with a regular posting schedule.
9. **Use Analytics**: Track performance metrics to refine your strategy.
10. **Stay Agile**: Continuously adapt to platform updates and changing trends.

Conclusion

TikTok's dynamic, trend-driven nature presents unique opportunities for brands to engage with younger audiences through creative and authentic content. By mastering the platform's culture, leveraging both organic and paid strategies, and continually experimenting, businesses can build a strong presence and capitalize on TikTok's immense potential. Whether you're driving brand awareness, encouraging user participation, or launching innovative ad campaigns, TikTok offers unparalleled possibilities to connect with today's digital-first consumers.

Chapter 10: YouTube

With over 2.5 billion monthly users, YouTube is the second-largest search engine globally, trailing only its parent company, Google[13]. Its focus on long-form video content makes it an invaluable platform for brands looking to engage audiences deeply, establish authority, and foster community. Whether you're creating tutorials, product reviews, or thought leadership content, YouTube offers the tools and audience reach to turn your channel into a powerhouse of marketing and engagement. This chapter explores how to effectively use YouTube to build trust, generate leads, and drive results.

Audience Demographics

YouTube's diverse user base makes it suitable for brands across industries:

- **Age Groups**: YouTube is widely popular across all age groups. While younger users dominate (18-34 years old), the platform also attracts a substantial number of users aged 35-54 and older.
- **Global Reach**: YouTube has a strong international presence, with content creators and audiences spanning the globe. Over 70% of watch time comes from outside the United States.
- **Content Preferences**: Viewers are drawn to a mix of educational content, entertainment, product reviews, tutorials, and vlogs, offering opportunities for various types of businesses to find their niche.

Understanding these demographics can help you tailor your content to match the preferences of your target audience.

Content Best Practices

Creating compelling YouTube videos requires a blend of creativity, strategy, and consistency. Here are key best practices:

1. **Focus on SEO**: As a search engine, YouTube's discoverability depends on how well you optimize your videos. Use relevant keywords in your video titles, descriptions, and tags to increase visibility.
2. **Create Eye-Catching Thumbnails**: Thumbnails are often the first thing viewers see. Ensure they are high-

quality, visually appealing, and include bold, readable text to encourage clicks.

3. **Stick to a Schedule**: Consistency is crucial on YouTube. Regular uploads (e.g., weekly or biweekly) help build viewer expectations and loyalty.

4. **Prioritize Value-Driven Content**: Focus on providing value to your audience through educational or entertaining videos. Avoid content that feels overly promotional.

5. **Engage Through Comments**: Respond to viewer comments to foster a sense of community and build loyalty. This interaction also signals to YouTube that your content is engaging.

Using YouTube for Organic Social Media Marketing

YouTube excels in organic social media marketing by allowing brands to create deep, meaningful connections with their audience through long-form content.

- **Educational Content**: Tutorials, how-to videos, and explainer videos are highly sought-after. For instance, a software company might create a series of videos demonstrating how to use their product effectively.

- **Thought Leadership**: Use YouTube to position your brand as an expert in your field. Share insights, industry trends, and solutions to common challenges faced by your target audience.
- **Behind-the-Scenes**: Give viewers a glimpse into your company culture, product development, or event preparation to humanize your brand.
- **Live Streaming**: Hosting live Q&A sessions, webinars, or product launches creates real-time engagement and deepens relationships with your audience.

Paid Social Media Functionality

YouTube Ads offers powerful tools for brands to amplify their reach and drive conversions. Here are some key features:

1. **Ad Formats**:
    - **Skippable In-Stream Ads**: Play before or during videos and allow viewers to skip after 5 seconds. Ideal for storytelling and driving brand awareness.
    - **Non-Skippable Ads**: Short ads (15-20 seconds) that viewers must watch before accessing their desired content.
    - **Bumper Ads**: Six-second, non-skippable ads designed for quick, impactful messages.

- Discovery Ads: Appear in YouTube search results or alongside related videos to attract viewers actively searching for content.
 - Masthead Ads: Premium placements on YouTube's homepage for maximum visibility.
2. **Targeting Options**: YouTube allows advertisers to target users based on demographics, interests, behaviors, and even specific video keywords. This ensures your ads reach the right audience at the right time.
3. **Remarketing**: Retarget users who have previously interacted with your content or website to nurture leads and encourage conversions.

Key Metrics to Measure Success

Tracking and analyzing performance metrics helps refine your strategy and achieve better results. Focus on these key metrics:

1. **Watch Time**: Measures the total amount of time viewers spend watching your videos. Longer watch times signal to YouTube that your content is engaging.
2. **Engagement**: Track likes, comments, shares, and subscribes to gauge how well your videos resonate with viewers.
3. **Click-Through Rate (CTR)**: Evaluate how effectively your thumbnails and titles attract clicks.

4. **Retention Rate**: Monitor how long viewers stay on your video. High retention rates indicate compelling content.
5. **Conversions**: For paid campaigns, track actions such as website visits, sign-ups, or purchases.
6. **Subscribers Gained**: Analyze how effectively your content encourages viewers to subscribe to your channel.

Checklist of 10 Tips to Be Successful on YouTube

1. **Define Your Niche**: Focus on a specific area of expertise to attract a loyal audience.
2. **Optimize for SEO**: Use relevant keywords in titles, descriptions, and tags to boost discoverability.
3. **Create Eye-Catching Thumbnails**: Design professional thumbnails that encourage viewers to click.
4. **Maintain a Posting Schedule**: Upload consistently to build audience expectations and loyalty.
5. **Focus on Quality Content**: Provide educational, entertaining, or inspirational value in every video.
6. **Engage with Your Audience**: Respond to comments and encourage interaction to foster community.
7. **Experiment with Formats**: Test different video styles, such as tutorials, interviews, or vlogs, to find what resonates best.

8. **Leverage Playlists**: Group related videos into playlists to keep viewers engaged and watching longer.
9. **Test Paid Ads**: Use YouTube Ads to amplify your reach and drive conversions.
10. **Analyze and Adapt**: Regularly review performance metrics to refine your strategy.

Conclusion

YouTube's unique combination of long-form content, searchability, and community-building features makes it a powerful platform for brands aiming to connect with their audience on a deeper level. By prioritizing SEO, creating high-value videos, and engaging consistently with viewers, you can build a loyal following and establish authority in your niche. Whether through organic content or targeted ad campaigns, YouTube offers unparalleled opportunities for growth, engagement, and ROI in the digital marketing landscape.

Chapter 11: X (formerly Twitter)

X (formerly known as Twitter) is a fast-paced platform ideal for real-time communication, thought leadership, and customer engagement. With 396 million monthly active users, X serves as a hub for sharing news, participating in trending conversations, and establishing a voice in global and industry-specific discussions. This chapter explores how to leverage X effectively, from curating impactful content to building campaigns that thrive in its dynamic environment.

Audience Demographics

X's audience is diverse, making it suitable for a range of businesses and marketing goals:

- **Age Groups**: X is most popular among users aged 18-34, with a growing base in the 35-49 demographic. It appeals to professionals, news enthusiasts, and individuals seeking real-time updates.
- **Global Reach**: The platform boasts a significant global presence, with users from North America, Europe, and Asia actively engaging with content.
- **Content Preferences**: X users are drawn to concise, informative content, breaking news, live event updates, and interactive campaigns. The platform attracts professionals, journalists, and organizations, making it a key space for thought leadership and industry engagement.

Content Best Practices

To succeed on X, brands need to craft concise, engaging, and timely content that resonates with its fast-moving audience:

1. **Be Concise**: The character limit (currently 280 characters) requires clear and compelling messaging. Use short, impactful statements and CTAs to grab attention.
2. **Use Visuals**: Tweets with images, GIFs, or videos consistently perform better. Visual content stands out in crowded feeds and encourages clicks.

3. **Leverage Hashtags**: Use relevant hashtags to increase visibility and join trending conversations. Branded hashtags are effective for campaigns or events.
4. **Curate and Share**: Position your brand as a thought leader by sharing insightful articles, blog posts, or data relevant to your industry.
5. **Engage in Real-Time**: Respond to breaking news, live-tweet events, and interact with followers to remain active in ongoing conversations.

Using X for Organic Social Media Marketing

Organic content on X is focused on fostering relationships, sharing timely updates, and participating in meaningful discussions:

- **Thought Leadership**: Share insights, opinions, and research to establish your brand as an authority in your industry. Position your X profile as a go-to resource for relevant expertise.
- **Customer Service**: Use X for direct customer interaction, responding to inquiries and resolving issues quickly. Many users turn to X for immediate responses from brands.

- **Community Building**: Start conversations around your brand by asking questions, creating polls, and participating in relevant discussions. This builds a sense of connection and engagement with followers.
- **Event Participation**: Live-tweet during industry events, product launches, or webinars to increase visibility and interact with attendees in real-time.

Paid Social Media Functionality

X Ads offer businesses the ability to amplify their reach, drive traffic, and achieve measurable goals through targeted campaigns.

1. **Ad Formats**:
    - **Promoted Tweets**: Boost specific tweets to appear in users' feeds, increasing visibility and engagement.
    - **Promoted Accounts**: Grow your follower base by promoting your profile to relevant users.
    - **Promoted Trends**: Feature your hashtag or topic in the trending section to drive massive awareness.
    - **Video Ads**: Leverage X's autoplay video ads for product demos, storytelling, or announcements.

2. **Targeting Options**: X allows advertisers to target audiences based on demographics, interests, keywords, and even the specific accounts users follow.
3. **Live Event Ads**: Advertisers can target users engaging with specific live events or trending topics, ensuring their content remains relevant and timely.
4. **Budget Flexibility**: Campaigns can be tailored to fit varying budgets, allowing businesses to scale their efforts based on performance.

Key Metrics to Measure Success

To evaluate your success on X, track the following metrics:

1. **Engagement Rate**: Measure likes, retweets, replies, and clicks to assess how well your content resonates with your audience.
2. **Impressions**: Track how many times your tweets are displayed in users' feeds.
3. **Follower Growth**: Monitor increases in your follower count to gauge your reach and influence.
4. **Click-Through Rate (CTR)**: Measure the effectiveness of your CTAs and links.
5. **Hashtag Performance**: Analyze the reach and engagement of branded or campaign-specific hashtags.

6. **Conversions**: For paid campaigns, track actions such as sign-ups, downloads, or purchases resulting from your ads.

Checklist of 10 Tips to Be Successful on X

1. **Define Your Voice**: Develop a consistent tone that aligns with your brand personality.
2. **Engage Regularly**: Post consistently and interact with followers to build relationships.
3. **Stay Timely**: Participate in trending topics or breaking news relevant to your industry.
4. **Use Visuals**: Incorporate images, videos, and GIFs to make your tweets stand out.
5. **Leverage Hashtags**: Use trending and branded hashtags strategically to boost visibility.
6. **Start Conversations**: Ask questions, create polls, and encourage user interaction.
7. **Respond Quickly**: Address comments, questions, and complaints promptly to show responsiveness.
8. **Experiment with Ad Formats**: Test different ad types to identify what drives the best results.
9. **Analyze Data**: Use X Analytics to track performance and refine your strategy.

10. **Monitor Competitors**: Observe how competitors use X and identify opportunities to differentiate your brand.

Conclusion

X's real-time nature, concise content format, and active user base make it a dynamic platform for brands looking to engage directly with their audience. By combining thought leadership, customer service, and participation in trending conversations, businesses can build a strong presence and foster meaningful connections. Whether through organic efforts or targeted ads, X offers a unique space to amplify your brand's voice and stay at the forefront of industry discussions. With a strategic approach, X can become an essential component of your social media marketing toolkit.

Chapter 12: LinkedIn

LinkedIn, with over 1 billion members, is the premier platform for professional networking and B2B marketing[14]. Its unique focus on business-related content and professional growth makes it an invaluable tool for brands seeking to reach decision-makers, generate leads, and build credibility. This chapter explores how to leverage LinkedIn's features, both organically and through paid strategies, to establish authority, foster connections, and achieve measurable results in the B2B space.

Audience Demographics

LinkedIn's user base is tailored for professionals, making it a perfect platform for B2B marketing and career-related content:

- **Professional Focus**: LinkedIn attracts a highly educated audience, with many users holding managerial and executive roles.
- **Age Groups**: The majority of users fall within the 25-49 age range, representing professionals in the early to mid-stages of their careers.
- **Industry Presence**: LinkedIn spans a wide range of industries, with strong representation in technology, finance, healthcare, education, and consulting.
- **Geographic Reach**: LinkedIn is used globally, with significant adoption in North America, Europe, and parts of Asia, offering opportunities for international marketing.

Understanding these demographics allows businesses to tailor content and campaigns to resonate with LinkedIn's professional audience.

Content Best Practices

To thrive on LinkedIn, brands must focus on creating high-value content that aligns with the platform's professional tone and audience interests:

1. **Share Thought Leadership**: Position your brand as an industry expert by sharing original research,

whitepapers, and insights. Thought leadership posts build credibility and attract engaged audiences.
2. **Provide Practical Value**: Post content that helps professionals solve problems, improve skills, or gain new knowledge. For example, case studies or "how-to" guides perform well.
3. **Incorporate Visuals and Video**: Posts with images or videos garner more attention in LinkedIn feeds. Use visuals to highlight key data points or create engaging video explainers.
4. **Leverage Articles and Newsletters**: Publish long-form articles to delve into industry trends or share in-depth analysis. LinkedIn's newsletter feature allows you to reach subscribers consistently.
5. **Engage with Comments**: Respond to comments on your posts to build relationships and demonstrate your brand's commitment to open dialogue.

Using LinkedIn for Organic Social Media Marketing

LinkedIn's organic tools are ideal for building relationships, showcasing expertise, and fostering professional growth:

- **Company Pages**: Maintain a strong presence by sharing regular updates, job postings, and achievements. Optimize your page with keywords and complete profiles to attract followers.
- **Employee Advocacy**: Encourage employees to share company content and updates, expanding reach through personal networks.
- **Groups and Communities**: Join or create LinkedIn Groups to participate in industry discussions and connect with niche audiences.
- **Networking Opportunities**: Use LinkedIn's messaging tools to engage directly with potential clients, partners, or influencers in your industry.
- **Consistency is Key**: Posting consistently (e.g., 3-5 times per week) ensures that your brand remains visible and relevant to followers.

Paid Social Media Functionality

LinkedIn Ads provide powerful tools for businesses to target decision-makers and drive measurable outcomes:

1. **Ad Formats**:
    - **Sponsored Content**: Promoted posts that appear in users' feeds to boost visibility and engagement.

- InMail Ads: Personalized messages delivered directly to users' LinkedIn inboxes, ideal for lead generation or event promotion.
- Text Ads: Simple, cost-effective ads displayed in the sidebar or at the top of the page.
- Dynamic Ads: Personalized ads that use profile data to tailor messages (e.g., showing a user's name or job title).
- Video Ads: Short videos for storytelling or product demonstrations.

2. **Targeting Capabilities**: LinkedIn's granular targeting options allow advertisers to reach users based on job title, company size, industry, seniority, and more. These tools make LinkedIn particularly effective for B2B campaigns focused on high-value prospects.
3. **Lead Generation Forms**: LinkedIn's native lead gen forms enable users to submit their contact information without leaving the platform, reducing friction and improving conversion rates.
4. **Account-Based Marketing (ABM)**: LinkedIn's targeting options support ABM strategies by allowing brands to focus campaigns on specific companies or key decision-makers.

Key Metrics to Measure Success

Tracking performance on LinkedIn ensures that your efforts are aligned with your goals. Focus on these metrics:

1. **Engagement Rate**: Measure likes, shares, comments, and clicks to gauge how well your content resonates with your audience.
2. **Impressions and Reach**: Monitor how many users see your posts and ads, as well as the frequency of visibility.
3. **Click-Through Rate (CTR)**: Evaluate how effectively your CTAs and headlines drive users to take action.
4. **Leads Generated**: For campaigns, track the number of leads captured through LinkedIn's lead generation forms or other landing pages.
5. **Follower Growth**: Analyze increases in your company page's followers to assess brand visibility.
6. **Conversions**: Track sales, registrations, or other desired outcomes from LinkedIn ads or content campaigns.

Checklist of 10 Tips to Be Successful on LinkedIn

1. **Optimize Your Profile**: Ensure your company page and employee profiles are complete and keyword-rich.
2. **Post Regularly**: Maintain a consistent posting schedule to stay visible and relevant.

3. **Focus on Thought Leadership**: Share original insights and research to position your brand as an industry expert.
4. **Leverage Visual Content**: Use images, infographics, and videos to capture attention in crowded feeds.
5. **Encourage Employee Advocacy**: Amplify your reach by having employees share content and engage with posts.
6. **Use Hashtags**: Incorporate relevant hashtags to increase the discoverability of your posts.
7. **Engage in Groups**: Participate actively in LinkedIn Groups to build relationships with niche audiences.
8. **Test Ad Formats**: Experiment with different ad types, such as Sponsored Content or InMail Ads, to find what works best.
9. **Monitor Analytics**: Use LinkedIn Analytics to track performance and refine your strategy.
10. **Personalize Outreach**: Send targeted messages to key connections to build relationships and drive engagement.

Conclusion

LinkedIn's focus on professional networking, thought leadership, and B2B marketing makes it a vital platform for brands looking to connect with decision-makers and establish authority. By leveraging both organic and paid strategies, businesses can build strong relationships, generate high-quality leads, and foster long-term growth. Whether sharing insights, engaging in discussions, or launching targeted campaigns, LinkedIn provides the tools to thrive in the competitive world of professional marketing.

Chapter 13: Snapchat

Snapchat, with its unique focus on ephemeral content and augmented reality (AR) features, has carved out a niche as a playful, interactive platform for connecting with younger audiences. With over 375 million daily active users and 850 million monthly active users, Snapchat excels at creating engaging, short-lived moments that encourage immediate interaction[15]. This chapter delves into how brands can leverage Snapchat's distinct features for marketing success, from building organic connections to utilizing its powerful paid advertising tools.

Audience Demographics

Snapchat's user base is predominantly young and tech-savvy, making it ideal for brands targeting Gen Z and millennials:

- **Age Groups**: The majority of Snapchat users are between the ages of 13 and 24, with strong engagement among users up to age 34.
- **Gender Distribution**: Snapchat has a nearly even split between male and female users, providing diverse opportunities for targeting.
- **Geographic Reach**: While most popular in North America and Europe, Snapchat also has growing audiences in other regions, including Asia and the Middle East.
- **User Behavior**: Snapchat users are highly active, sending over 4 billion snaps daily and spending an average of 30+ minutes per day on the app.

Understanding these demographics can help brands tailor their messaging and campaigns to resonate with Snapchat's youthful and engaged audience.

Content Best Practices

Snapchat's format requires brands to focus on creativity, immediacy, and visual storytelling. Here are key content strategies:

1. **Leverage Storytelling**: Use Snapchat Stories to share behind-the-scenes glimpses, product demos, or event

highlights. Stories create a sense of urgency as they disappear after 24 hours.

2. **Embrace AR Filters and Lenses**: Create branded AR filters and lenses to encourage playful user interaction with your brand. These features are especially popular during holidays, events, and product launches.

3. **Keep It Authentic**: Snapchat thrives on authenticity. Content that feels raw and spontaneous often performs better than overly polished visuals.

4. **Use Vertical Video**: Ensure all video content is optimized for vertical viewing, the default orientation for Snapchat users.

5. **Incorporate Text and Stickers**: Enhance engagement by adding captions, emojis, and stickers that align with your brand's personality.

Using Snapchat for Organic Social Media Marketing

Organic marketing on Snapchat focuses on building connections, fostering engagement, and creating memorable experiences:

- **Snapchat Stories**: Share a series of short videos or photos to create a cohesive narrative. For example, a

fashion brand might showcase a day in the life of a designer.
- **Behind-the-Scenes Content**: Give followers an exclusive look at your team, events, or production process to build transparency and trust.
- **Interactive Polls and Quizzes**: Use Snapchat's interactive features to engage your audience in a fun and participatory way.
- **Collaborations with Creators**: Partner with Snapchat influencers to reach their established audiences organically.

Paid Social Media Functionality

Snapchat offers a variety of paid advertising tools that enable brands to amplify their reach and achieve specific business objectives:

1. **Ad Formats**:
    - **Snap Ads**: Full-screen, vertical video ads that appear between Stories and can include swipe-up CTAs for website visits or app downloads.
    - **Story Ads**: Appear in Snapchat's Discover section, where users actively explore content.
    - **Collection Ads**: Showcase multiple products within a single ad, ideal for e-commerce brands.

- **AR Lenses and Filters**: Branded AR experiences that users can apply to their photos and videos.
- **Commercials**: Non-skippable ads up to six seconds long, ensuring guaranteed visibility.
2. **Targeting Options**: Snapchat Ads Manager allows advertisers to target users by age, gender, location, interests, and behaviors. Advanced options like Lookalike Audiences help brands reach new potential customers similar to their existing audience.
3. **Dynamic Ads**: Automatically generate personalized ads based on your product catalog, making it easier to scale campaigns for e-commerce.
4. **Geofilters**: Location-based filters that users can apply when snapping in specific areas, perfect for local promotions or event marketing.

Key Metrics to Measure Success

To evaluate the effectiveness of your Snapchat marketing efforts, focus on these metrics:

1. **Story Views**: Track how many users watch your Stories to assess reach and engagement.
2. **Swipe-Ups**: Measure the number of users who swipe up on your ads or Stories to visit a website, app, or landing page.

3. **Engagement Rate**: Analyze user interactions with your AR lenses, filters, or other interactive content.
4. **Conversions**: For paid campaigns, monitor app installs, purchases, or other desired actions driven by your ads.
5. **Completion Rate**: Evaluate how many users watch your ads or Stories to the end, indicating how engaging your content is.
6. **Time Spent**: Track how long users interact with your lenses or filters to gauge their impact.

Checklist of 10 Tips to Be Successful on Snapchat

1. **Understand Your Audience**: Tailor content to Snapchat's younger demographic and their preferences.
2. **Be Creative**: Use AR lenses, filters, and engaging visuals to capture attention.
3. **Embrace Ephemeral Content**: Leverage Stories and Snaps to create a sense of urgency and exclusivity.
4. **Keep It Authentic**: Avoid overly polished content; focus on relatable and spontaneous moments.
5. **Use Interactive Features**: Incorporate polls, quizzes, and swipe-up CTAs to boost engagement.
6. **Experiment with Ad Formats**: Test different ad types, such as Story Ads and Collection Ads, to find what works best.

7. **Collaborate with Influencers**: Partner with Snapchat creators to expand your reach organically.
8. **Leverage Geofilters**: Use location-based filters for local events or promotions.
9. **Analyze Performance**: Use Snapchat Analytics to refine your strategy based on metrics like views and conversions.
10. **Stay Updated on Trends**: Monitor Snapchat trends and features to ensure your content remains fresh and relevant.

Conclusion

Snapchat's emphasis on ephemeral content, creativity, and interactivity makes it a unique platform for engaging younger audiences and building brand awareness. By combining organic strategies like Stories and AR filters with targeted paid campaigns, brands can create memorable experiences that drive meaningful results. Whether you're showcasing behind-the-scenes moments, launching a playful AR lens, or running a geofilter campaign, Snapchat offers endless possibilities for connecting with audiences in a fun and authentic way.

Chapter 14: Other Channels to Consider

While the major platforms dominate the social media landscape, there are several emerging or niche platforms that marketers should consider, depending on their industry and audience. Let's explore several of these.

Pinterest: A Visual and E-Commerce Powerhouse

Pinterest is a visual discovery platform with a strong focus on inspiration, creativity, and e-commerce. With over 400 million monthly active users, Pinterest attracts individuals seeking ideas for home décor, fashion, DIY projects, travel, and recipes. The platform's unique appeal lies in its highly intent-driven audience—users often come to Pinterest with the goal of discovering new products, making it ideal for marketers looking to drive traffic and conversions.

The platform is particularly effective for e-commerce brands, thanks to features like Product Pins, which enable direct shopping, and Pinterest Trends, which provides insights into emerging interests among users. Pinterest's demographics skew slightly female, with a strong presence among millennials and Gen Z. For marketers in industries such as interior design, fashion, or wellness, Pinterest offers a golden opportunity to showcase visually stunning content and capture the attention of a highly engaged audience. The ability to optimize content for search within the platform further enhances visibility, making Pinterest a valuable tool for long-term content marketing strategies.

Threads: A New Platform for Real-Time Conversations

Threads, Meta's newest text-based social media platform, is quickly gaining traction as a space for real-time interactions and community building. Designed as an extension of Instagram, Threads blends features from both Instagram and X (formerly Twitter), offering users a text-first experience with integrated visual elements. Its rapid growth is fueled by its seamless connection to Instagram, allowing users to migrate their existing follower base and maintain consistent branding across platforms.

Marketers can leverage Threads to participate in real-time conversations, share quick updates, and foster closer connections with their audience. The platform's text-based nature makes it an excellent choice for brands aiming to establish thought leadership or engage in interactive Q&A sessions. While still in its early stages, Threads' integration with Meta's ecosystem provides robust opportunities for cross-platform marketing, enabling brands to combine visual storytelling on Instagram with dynamic, conversational content on Threads.

Reddit: A Niche Marketer's Playground

Reddit is a community-driven platform with over 50 million daily active users who engage in discussions across thousands of specialized forums, known as subreddits. Unlike traditional social media platforms, Reddit's strength lies in its hyper-engaged user base, which seeks authentic conversations and highly specific content. This makes it particularly valuable for marketers targeting niche industries, technical audiences, or communities with shared interests.

Marketers can use Reddit to establish authority by participating in discussions, answering questions, or sharing insights relevant to their industry. The platform's subreddit structure allows brands to directly target audiences with highly relevant messaging. For example, a technology company might engage with users in r/technology or r/programming to showcase expertise and generate leads. Additionally, Reddit Ads offer precise targeting based on subreddit interests, enabling marketers to reach audiences that are difficult to target on other platforms. However, success on Reddit requires a careful, non-promotional approach, as its community values authenticity and transparency.

Bluesky: A Decentralized Alternative for Networking

Bluesky, a decentralized social network founded by former Twitter CEO Jack Dorsey, is an emerging platform focused on user ownership and open protocols. While still in its early adoption phase, Bluesky is attracting users who prioritize privacy, freedom from algorithms, and control over their online identities. The platform's structure allows for a more personalized user experience, making it appealing to industry professionals and niche communities.

Marketers might find Bluesky valuable for connecting with forward-thinking audiences or building early traction within specific industries. By positioning themselves as early adopters, brands can establish credibility and gain visibility among tech-savvy users who appreciate innovation and decentralization. While Bluesky's user base is currently small compared to major platforms, its emphasis on decentralization and user control aligns with growing consumer concerns about privacy and data ownership, making it a platform to watch.

Industry-Specific Social Networks

In addition to mainstream platforms, industry-specific social networks provide unique opportunities for marketers to engage with specialized audiences. Platforms like Behance (for creative professionals), Houzz (for home improvement and design), and ResearchGate (for academics and researchers) cater to professionals within specific fields. These networks allow brands to connect directly with industry insiders, showcase expertise, and build relationships in a highly targeted environment.

For example, a furniture brand might use Houzz to engage with interior designers and homeowners, sharing product catalogs and participating in discussions about design trends. Similarly, a marketing firm might leverage Behance to highlight its creative portfolio and attract potential clients. While these platforms may have smaller user bases compared to major networks, their targeted audiences provide high-value opportunities for brands to reach decision-makers and establish themselves as leaders within their industry.

Conclusion

By understanding the unique characteristics and user bases of these platforms, marketers can expand their reach and tailor their strategies to tap into niche communities and emerging social networks. Each platform offers distinct advantages that, when aligned with a brand's goals, can yield significant returns.

Each social media platform offers distinct advantages and challenges, and successful marketing depends on understanding the nuances of each one. Whether you're leveraging Facebook's vast user base, Instagram's visual storytelling, TikTok's viral trends, YouTube's long-form video, or LinkedIn's professional networks, tailoring your content and strategy to fit the platform is key to maximizing results. Emerging platforms like Pinterest and Threads offer additional opportunities for brands to reach new audiences, depending on their industry and goals.

Chapter 15: Social Commerce

Social commerce is revolutionizing the way consumers shop, allowing them to make purchases directly within social media platforms. This integration of e-commerce and social media provides a seamless shopping experience, reducing the friction between discovering a product and completing a purchase. Platforms such as Instagram, TikTok, and Pinterest have embraced social commerce, creating features that enable brands to sell products directly through posts, videos, and pins. With the global social commerce market projected to reach $1.2 trillion by 2025, understanding how to leverage these platforms is key to staying competitive in the digital landscape.

The Rise of Social Commerce

Social commerce has emerged as a powerful trend, driven by changing consumer behaviors and advances in social media platforms. The convenience of shopping without leaving a social app, combined with the influence of user-generated content, has made it easier than ever for consumers to make purchase decisions based on social recommendations, influencer endorsements, and viral trends.

1. **Instagram**: Instagram has been at the forefront of social commerce innovation. With features like Instagram Shopping and shoppable posts, brands can tag products directly in their content, allowing users to browse and purchase items without leaving the app. Instagram also integrates with Shopify and other e-commerce platforms, streamlining the checkout process. According to Instagram, 70% of shopping enthusiasts turn to the platform for product discovery, making it a prime channel for social commerce.
2. **TikTok**: Known for its viral, short-form videos, TikTok has become a major player in social commerce. TikTok's algorithm-driven feed surfaces products in creative and engaging ways, often leveraging user-generated content and trends. The platform's partnership with Shopify allows businesses to sell products directly from their TikTok profiles, and the "TikTok Made Me Buy It" phenomenon highlights how viral content can translate into real sales. TikTok's strength lies in its ability to create viral moments that drive instant shopping interest.

3. **Pinterest**: Pinterest offers a highly visual and discovery-driven shopping experience, making it an ideal platform for social commerce. With its integration of shoppable pins, users can find inspiration and immediately act on it by purchasing products. Pinterest's advanced search functionality allows users to find specific products, while its AI-powered recommendations surface products that match users' tastes. As of 2021, Pinterest reported that 89% of its users were on the platform for purchase inspiration, positioning it as a strong player in the social commerce space.

Strategies for Social Commerce Success

To succeed in social commerce, brands need to focus on creating engaging content, simplifying the shopping experience, and leveraging influencers to drive sales. Below are some strategies to optimize your social commerce efforts:

1. **Optimizing Content for Social Commerce**: To capture attention in the fast-paced world of social media, content needs to be visually appealing and instantly engaging. Brands should create high-quality images, videos, and product showcases that highlight the key benefits of their products. On platforms like Instagram and TikTok, creating content that aligns with trending challenges, hashtags, and aesthetics can significantly boost visibility.

2. **Creating Shoppable Posts**: Shoppable posts are the backbone of social commerce. Platforms like Instagram and Pinterest allow businesses to tag products in their content, making it easy for users to click through and purchase directly. Brands should ensure that these posts feel natural and organic, rather than overly promotional. For example, fashion brands can showcase products in real-life settings or styled by influencers, making the experience more relatable and less like traditional advertising.

3. **Leveraging Influencers**: Influencer marketing is a key driver of social commerce success. Influencers, especially those with strong engagement and a loyal following, can drive significant sales by showcasing products in authentic ways. Partnering with influencers who align with your brand's values and target audience is crucial for ensuring the content feels genuine. Influencers often help create a sense of urgency or exclusivity around a product, which can spur quicker purchase decisions.

4. **Building a Seamless Checkout Experience**: Reducing friction in the buying process is essential for maximizing conversions in social commerce. A seamless checkout experience—where users can complete a purchase without leaving the platform—can dramatically improve conversion rates. Features like Instagram's in-app

checkout or TikTok's direct Shopify integration allow customers to complete purchases with just a few clicks, making the process intuitive and fast.

5. **Encouraging User-Generated Content (UGC)**: Social commerce thrives on the authenticity of user-generated content. Encouraging customers to share photos and videos of your products not only increases engagement but also provides social proof, which builds trust among potential buyers. Brands can incentivize UGC by hosting challenges, offering discounts for tagged posts, or featuring customer content on their profiles.

Conclusion

Social commerce is reshaping the future of e-commerce, blending the discovery-driven nature of social media with the immediacy of online shopping. Platforms like Instagram, TikTok, and Pinterest have developed robust tools that allow brands to create a seamless shopping experience, from product discovery to checkout. By optimizing content, leveraging influencers, and building a frictionless purchase process, businesses can effectively capitalize on the growing trend of social commerce and tap into a new era of digital shopping.

This shift represents a significant opportunity for brands to drive sales directly through the platforms where their customers are spending the most time, transforming social media from a marketing channel into a complete commerce engine.

Chapter 16: Content Creation Best Practices for Social Media

Creating compelling, engaging, and authentic content is at the core of any successful social media strategy. In today's digital landscape, consumers are inundated with content, making it more critical than ever for brands to craft content that resonates with their audience, captures attention, and encourages interaction. From understanding your target audience to mastering the nuances of storytelling and content scheduling, creating impactful social media content requires a blend of creativity and strategy.

Understanding Your Audience

The foundation of any effective social media content strategy starts with a deep understanding of your audience. Before creating content, it's essential to conduct thorough audience research to identify who your followers are, what they care about, and how they interact with content. One of the best ways to achieve this is by developing audience personas—fictional representations of your ideal customers. These personas should include demographic information such as age, gender, occupation, and interests, as well as psychographic details like values, pain points, and motivations.

By understanding your audience's preferences, brands can tailor content that speaks directly to them. For example, research may reveal that a fitness brand's audience is primarily young adults who are highly engaged with health and wellness tips. This insight allows the brand to create content focused on fitness challenges, workout routines, and nutritional advice, rather than generic promotional posts.

Actionable Tips:

- Use social media analytics tools (such as Facebook Insights or Twitter Analytics) to gather data on your followers' demographics, behaviors, and preferences.
- Survey your audience to learn about their interests, challenges, and the type of content they enjoy.

- Develop 2-3 audience personas that reflect your key customer segments, and use these personas to guide your content creation.

Creating Engaging and Authentic Content

Creating content that is both engaging and authentic is critical for building trust and fostering deeper connections with your audience. In a world where consumers crave transparency, authenticity can make your brand stand out. This means avoiding overly promotional content and focusing on storytelling, visuals, and relatable experiences.

1. **Storytelling**: Great storytelling helps humanize your brand and create an emotional connection with your audience. Whether it's sharing the story behind your brand's founding, showcasing customer success stories, or highlighting employees' experiences, stories allow followers to see the human side of your business. Brands like Apple and Nike excel in storytelling by focusing on the experiences and emotions behind their products rather than just the products themselves.
2. **High-Quality Visuals**: Social media is a highly visual medium, and high-quality visuals are key to catching attention in a crowded feed. Platforms like Instagram

and Pinterest prioritize visually appealing content, but even on text-driven platforms like Twitter, posts with images receive significantly higher engagement. Investing in professional photography, well-designed graphics, or eye-catching infographics can elevate your brand's presence and credibility.

3. **The Power of Video**: Video content consistently outperforms other types of posts in terms of engagement. Videos can range from short, snackable clips on TikTok and Instagram Reels to longer, in-depth content on YouTube or Facebook. Live videos, in particular, are growing in popularity, as they offer real-time interaction and an authentic feel. According to research, 80% of users prefer watching live videos from a brand over reading a blog post

Actionable Tips:

- Use storytelling frameworks like the "Hero's Journey" to structure your brand's stories.
- Invest in high-quality visuals, whether through professional design tools or by collaborating with talented creators.
- Create a mix of short-form and long-form video content, and experiment with live videos to engage with your audience in real-time.

Scheduling and Frequency

Knowing when and how often to post on social media is a crucial part of maintaining relevance without overwhelming your audience. Each social media platform has peak times when users are most active, and understanding these patterns allows you to maximize your content's visibility.

1. **Best Times to Post**: The optimal time to post can vary depending on the platform and your audience. For example, studies show that Instagram posts tend to perform best during lunch hours (11 AM - 1 PM) and in the evening (7 PM - 9 PM), while LinkedIn posts are more effective during work hours (8 AM - 2 PM). Testing and analyzing the performance of your posts during different times can help refine your posting schedule.
2. **Posting Frequency**: Posting frequency can significantly impact engagement rates. However, the right frequency will depend on the platform and your audience's preferences. On platforms like Twitter, where content has a short shelf life, posting multiple times a day may be necessary. On Instagram or LinkedIn, posting 3-5 times per week may be more appropriate. It's essential to strike a balance between posting consistently and avoiding content fatigue.

Actionable Tips:

- Use social media management tools (like Buffer or Hootsuite) to schedule posts in advance and ensure consistency.
- Analyze your content's performance by experimenting with different posting times and frequencies.
- Maintain a content calendar to ensure your posts are aligned with campaigns, product launches, and holidays.

Conclusion

Creating successful social media content requires a deep understanding of your audience, a commitment to authenticity, and a strategic approach to scheduling and posting. By focusing on audience personas, crafting engaging stories, using high-quality visuals, and maintaining a consistent posting schedule, brands can build meaningful connections with their followers and enhance their social media presence. As the digital landscape continues to evolve, staying agile and data-driven in your approach to content creation will be key to standing out and achieving sustained success across platforms.

Chapter 17: Future Trends in Social Media Marketing to Consider

As social media continues to evolve at an accelerated pace, marketers must stay ahead of emerging trends to remain competitive. From the increasing use of artificial intelligence (AI) to the rise of the metaverse, the social media landscape is set to undergo significant transformations in the coming years. These changes will impact how brands engage with audiences, how content is created, and how social platforms integrate with broader digital experiences. In this section, we will explore key trends shaping the future of social media marketing.

The Growth of AI and Automation

AI is rapidly transforming how businesses approach social media marketing. From chatbots to personalized content recommendations, AI enables marketers to automate processes and deliver more targeted, efficient campaigns.

1. **Chatbots and Customer Service**: AI-powered chatbots have become a standard feature for brands looking to offer real-time customer support on social platforms like Facebook Messenger and WhatsApp. These bots can handle everything from answering common customer queries to assisting with online shopping, streamlining the customer journey while reducing response times. Gartner predicts that by 2025, 80% of customer service interactions will be handled by AI-driven systems, further underscoring the importance of adopting chatbot technology.

2. **Content Generation and Personalization**: AI is also being leveraged to generate content at scale. Tools like ChatGPT and Copy.ai allow brands to create personalized posts, captions, and ad copy quickly, reducing the workload for content creators while maintaining high levels of relevance for different audience segments. As AI advances, brands will be able to use machine learning algorithms to analyze past engagement data and optimize content for better performance.

3. **Audience Targeting and Automation Tools**: AI-driven audience targeting has already revolutionized social media advertising. Platforms like Facebook and Instagram use AI to refine ad delivery, ensuring that ads reach the most relevant users based on their behaviors, preferences, and interactions. Automation tools, such as HubSpot, Hootsuite, and Sprout Social, further streamline the process by scheduling posts, tracking performance, and delivering data-driven insights on what content is resonating with audiences.

Looking Ahead: As AI and automation technologies continue to advance, brands that harness these tools effectively will be able to scale their social media efforts, optimize engagement, and deliver highly personalized experiences at a lower cost.

The Metaverse and Social Media

The concept of the metaverse—an immersive, digital world where users can interact in virtual environments—has gained significant attention, particularly with Meta (formerly Facebook) leading the charge. The integration of virtual reality (VR) and augmented reality (AR) into social experiences is expected to redefine how brands interact with audiences.

1. **Meta's Vision for the Metaverse**: Meta's investment in the metaverse is set to create a virtual space where users can work, play, shop, and socialize in a fully immersive environment. In the future, social platforms could transition into more interactive, 3D spaces, offering brands new ways to engage with consumers. Imagine virtual showrooms, 3D product demos, or interactive brand experiences where users can "try on" products virtually before making a purchase.

2. **Opportunities for Brand Engagement**: The metaverse presents exciting opportunities for social commerce and branded experiences. Retailers, for example, could create virtual storefronts where users can browse products as if they were in a physical store. Fashion brands are already experimenting with virtual fashion shows, while entertainment companies are hosting virtual concerts and events.

3. **AR and VR Features**: Many platforms have already begun integrating AR and VR features. Snapchat's AR lenses and Instagram's AR filters allow users to interact with brands in new, creative ways. As VR hardware becomes more affordable, these immersive technologies will likely become a standard feature across social platforms, enhancing user engagement and brand loyalty.

Looking Ahead: While the full realization of the metaverse may still be a few years away, brands should start exploring how they can experiment with AR and VR to deliver more immersive, interactive experiences to their audiences.

New Features and Algorithm Changes

Social media platforms are constantly evolving, with new features and algorithm updates influencing how brands reach and engage users. Staying up to date with these changes is crucial for marketers who want to maintain relevance and maximize their content's visibility.

1. **Algorithm Updates**: Social media algorithms are becoming more sophisticated, prioritizing content that generates meaningful interactions and keeps users on the platform longer. For example, Facebook and Instagram's algorithms now favor content that sparks conversations in comments, while TikTok's algorithm is designed to surface content that's likely to go viral based on engagement and watch time.
2. **Emerging Features**: Platforms are continually rolling out new features to enhance user experience and keep brands engaged. Instagram recently expanded its shopping capabilities with product tags and in-app checkout, while TikTok introduced "TikTok Shopping" to integrate e-commerce more seamlessly. Additionally,

LinkedIn has introduced new content formats such as LinkedIn Live and LinkedIn Stories, allowing brands to engage with professional audiences in more dynamic ways.

3. **Social Audio**: The rise of social audio platforms, such as Clubhouse, and features like Twitter Spaces highlight the growing popularity of voice-based content. These platforms provide brands with opportunities to engage in real-time, voice-driven conversations, host live discussions, and participate in thought leadership in a more intimate and interactive format.

Looking Ahead: Marketers will need to stay agile and adapt quickly to new platform updates and features. Those who can leverage these changes early will be better positioned to drive engagement and reach new audiences effectively.

Conclusion

The future of social media marketing is set to be defined by rapid technological advancements and evolving user behaviors. AI and automation are making it easier for brands to deliver personalized content at scale, while the rise of the metaverse is opening up new avenues for immersive, interactive experiences. Meanwhile, ongoing algorithm updates and the introduction of new features are constantly reshaping how brands connect with audiences. By staying ahead of these trends and being proactive in adopting new technologies, marketers can ensure their brands remain competitive in an increasingly complex digital landscape.

Epilogue

The world of social media is in constant flux, driven by rapid technological advancements, shifting consumer behaviors, and emerging platforms. Throughout this book, we have explored how social media marketing has evolved, from the early days of organic reach to the sophisticated tools and strategies available today. As businesses continue to navigate this dynamic environment, adaptability remains the key to long-term success.

The Power of Integration and Strategy

One of the central themes discussed is the importance of integrating social media into a larger marketing strategy. Social media is not an isolated channel—it works best when it complements other aspects of marketing, such as email campaigns, content marketing, and paid media. The best-performing brands today use social media to amplify their broader marketing efforts, offering personalized experiences, retargeting customers, and creating consistent messaging across all touchpoints.

The Shift Toward Personalization and Engagement

Another core theme is the shift from generic content to highly personalized, engaging interactions. Today's consumers expect more than just advertisements—they want content that resonates with their values, needs, and interests. Whether through community building, storytelling, or influencer collaborations, successful brands are those that foster meaningful relationships with their audience. The rise of AI and automation in audience targeting, content personalization, and customer service has made it easier than ever to deliver these tailored experiences at scale.

The Rise of Social Commerce

Social commerce has become a significant part of the marketing landscape, blending e-commerce with social engagement. Platforms like Instagram, TikTok, and Pinterest are pioneering this trend, enabling brands to meet consumers where they spend their time and make purchases in a few simple clicks. As shopping continues to integrate into social experiences, businesses must adapt to these new consumer behaviors by making their content and products instantly shoppable and accessible.

Staying Ahead of Trends

As we look to the future, it's clear that social media will continue to evolve. The rapid adoption of AI, the emergence of the metaverse, and ongoing changes in algorithms are just a few factors shaping the next wave of social media marketing. To remain competitive, brands need to be proactive in testing new features, tools, and platforms. Innovation in social media marketing often stems from early adoption, and those who can embrace change while staying true to their brand values will stand out.

The Importance of Continuous Learning and Experimentation

The only constant in social media marketing is change. To thrive in this ever-evolving space, businesses must commit to continuous learning. This means staying informed on the latest platform updates, trends, and best practices. It also means continually testing new strategies and embracing a mindset of experimentation. Social media provides real-time feedback, allowing marketers to quickly adjust and refine their approach based on performance data.

The future of social media marketing is bright, filled with new opportunities for brands to connect with their audience in meaningful ways. By staying adaptable, informed, and customer-focused, businesses can navigate this evolving landscape with confidence and continue to thrive in the digital age.

About the Author

Greg Kihlström is a best-selling author, speaker, and entrepreneur and serves as an advisor and consultant to top companies on marketing technology, marketing operations, customer experience, and digital transformation initiatives. He has worked with some of the world's top brands, including Adidas, Coca-Cola, FedEx, HP, Marriott, Nationwide, Victoria's Secret, and Toyota.

He is a multiple-time Co-Founder and C-level leader, leading his digital experience agency to be acquired by the largest independent marketing agency in the DC region in 2017, successfully exited an HR technology platform provider he co-founded in 2020, and led a SaaS startup to be acquired by a leading edge computing company in 2021. He currently advises and sits on the Board of a marketing technology startup.

In addition to his experience as an entrepreneur and leader, he earned his MBA, is currently a doctoral candidate for a DBA in Business Intelligence, and teaches several courses and workshops as a member of the School of Marketing Faculty at the Association of National Advertisers. He has served on the Virginia Tech Pamplin College of Business Marketing Mentorship Advisory Board, the University of Richmond's CX Advisory Board, and was the founding Chair of the American Advertising Federation's National Innovation Committee. Greg is Lean Six Sigma Black Belt certified, is an Agile Certified Coach (ICP-ACC) and holds a certification in Business Agility (ICP-BAF).

Greg has had multiple best-selling books, including his 10-part Agile Brand Guides series on marketing technology platforms and practices. His most recent book, the best-selling House of the Customer (2023), discusses the 1:1 personalized customer experience of the future and how brands can organize the people, processes, and platforms that enable it. His award-winning podcast, The Agile Brand with Greg Kihlström, now in its 6th year with over 450 episodes and 2 million downloads, discusses brand strategy, marketing, and customer experience with some of the world's leading experts and leaders.

Greg is a contributing writer to Fast Company, Forbes, MarTech, CustomerThink, and CMSWire and has been featured in publications such as Advertising Age and The Washington

Post. Greg has been named #1 on its list of the Top Global Marketing Thought Leaders by Thinkers 360, was named one of ICMI's Top 25 CX Thought Leaders two years in a row, and a DC Inno 50 on Fire as a DC trendsetter in Marketing. He's also participated as a speaker at global industry events and has guest lectured at prominent universities and colleges.

Greg lives in Alexandria, Virginia, with his wife, Lindsey, and their three Roombas.

Appendix I: Social Media Marketing Terms Glossary

- **Algorithm**

A set of rules used by social media platforms to determine which content is shown to users based on their behavior, preferences, and engagement patterns.

- **Augmented Reality (AR)**

A technology that overlays digital elements, such as filters or 3D objects, onto the real world, often used in social media apps like Snapchat and Instagram.

- **Audience Demographics**

Characteristics of a target audience, such as age, gender, location, and interests, used to tailor content and advertising strategies.

- **Brand Awareness**

The extent to which a brand is recognized by potential customers and associated with specific products or services.

- **Branded Hashtag**

A custom hashtag created by a brand for campaigns or promotions to increase visibility and encourage user-generated content.

- **Call-to-Action (CTA)**

A prompt encouraging users to take a specific action, such as "Shop Now," "Learn More," or "Subscribe."

- **Click-Through Rate (CTR)**

The percentage of users who click on a link or ad after viewing it, used to measure the effectiveness of campaigns.

- **Conversion Rate**

The percentage of users who complete a desired action, such as making a purchase or signing up for a newsletter, after interacting with social media content.

- **Cost Per Click (CPC)**

The amount an advertiser pays each time a user clicks on their ad, commonly used in social media advertising.

- **Cost Per Thousand Impressions (CPM)**

The cost of displaying an ad to 1,000 users. Used to measure brand awareness campaigns.

- **Discovery Ads**

Ads designed to appear in search results, alongside relevant content, or in platform discovery feeds, such as on YouTube or Snapchat.

- **Engagement Rate**

A metric that measures interactions with content, including likes, comments, shares, and clicks, relative to total impressions or followers.

- **Ephemeral Content**

Temporary content that disappears after a set period, such as Instagram Stories or Snapchat Snaps.

- **Hashtag**

A keyword or phrase preceded by the "#" symbol, used to categorize and increase the discoverability of posts.

- **Impressions**

The number of times a post, ad, or piece of content is displayed to users, regardless of whether it's clicked.

- **Influencer Marketing**

A strategy that involves partnering with individuals who have a strong social media presence to promote products or services.

- **Lookalike Audience**

A targeted advertising audience created by identifying users with similar characteristics to an existing customer base.

- **Organic Reach**

The number of people who see a post or content without paid promotion.

Agile Brand Guide: Social Media Marketing

- **Paid Social**

The use of paid advertising on social media platforms to amplify reach, drive traffic, and achieve specific marketing goals.

- **Pinned Post**

A post that is fixed to the top of a social media profile or page to ensure visibility.

- **Platform-Specific Features**

Unique tools and functionalities offered by individual social media platforms, such as Reels on Instagram or AR Lenses on Snapchat.

- **Retargeting**

A strategy that serves ads to users who have previously interacted with a brand's website or social media content.

- **Social Commerce**

The use of social media platforms to sell products or services directly through features like Shoppable Posts or integrated checkout options.

- **Social Listening**

The process of monitoring social media channels for mentions, trends, or conversations about a brand, competitors, or industry.

- **Sponsored Content**

Paid posts or ads that appear in a user's feed and are designed to look like organic content.

- **Stories**

A form of ephemeral content that disappears after 24 hours, available on platforms like Instagram, Facebook, and Snapchat.

- **Swipe-Up Feature**

A feature in Stories that allows users to access a link by swiping up, commonly used for driving traffic to a website or landing page.

- **User-Generated Content (UGC)**

Content created by customers or followers that features a brand's products or services, often shared by the brand to build authenticity and trust.

- **Vertical Video**

Video content shot in a vertical orientation, optimized for mobile viewing on platforms like TikTok, Instagram, and Snapchat.

- **Viral Content**

Content that gains rapid popularity and widespread sharing across social media platforms due to its engaging or relatable nature.

References

1 Eric Eldon, August 4, 2008. "Friendster raises $20 million, nabs a Googler to be CEO Archived August 24, 2017, at the Wayback Machine" VentureBeat. Retrieved December 4, 2008.

2 Molloy, Fran (March 27, 2008). "Internet connectivity " Science Features (ABC Science)". Abc.net.au. Archived from the original on November 26, 2020. Retrieved October 19, 2012.

3 Pete Cashmore (July 11, 2006). "MySpace, America's Number One". Mashable.com. Archived from the original on May 25, 2010. Retrieved July 24, 2010.

4 https://historycooperative.org/the-history-of-social-media/

5 https://www.business-standard.com/article/international/mark-zuckerberg-bought-instagram-as-it-was-a-threat-to-facebook-120073000324_1.html#:~:text=Facebook%20bought%20Instagram%20for%20%241,a%20company%20with%2013%20employees

6 https://historycooperative.org/the-history-of-social-media/

7 https://greekreporter.com/2023/08/07/myspace-fall/

8 https://www.britannica.com/topic/Myspace

9 https://greekreporter.com/2023/08/07/myspace-fall/

10 Dean, B. (2023, September 5). *Facebook user & growth statistics to know in 2024*. Backlinko. Retrieved December 8, 2024, from https://backlinko.com/facebook-users

11 SOAX. (2023, November 1). *How many users does Instagram have?* SOAX. Retrieved December 8, 2024, from https://soax.com/research/how-many-users-does-instagram-have

12 Charle Agency. (2024, September 8). *Top 23 TikTok statistics & facts you need to know!* Charle Agency. Retrieved December 8, 2024, from https://www.charleagency.com/articles/tiktok-statistics/

13 SEO.ai. (2024, December 2). *How many people use YouTube? Statistics & facts (2025)*. SEO.ai. Retrieved December 8, 2024, from https://seo.ai/blog/how-many-people-use-youtube

14 LinkedIn. (n.d.). *About LinkedIn*. Retrieved December 8, 2024, from https://about.linkedin.com/

15 Singh, S. (2024, October 15). *How many people use Snapchat (active users 2024)*. Demand Sage. Retrieved December 8, 2024, from https://www.demandsage.com/snapchat-users/

www.ingramcontent.com/pod-product-compliance
Lightning Source LLC
Chambersburg PA
CBHW071030240526
45469CB00006BD/2157